The KGB

WORLD ESPIONAGE

The KGB
The Russian Secret Police from the Days of the Czars to the Present

Graham Yost

Facts On File
New York • Oxford

The KGB: The Russian Secret Police from the Days of the Czars to the Present

Facts On File, Inc.
460 Park Avenue South
New York, New York 10016

Library of Congress Cataloging-in-Publication Data

Yost, Graham.
    The KGB: the Russian secret police from the czars to the present.
    (World Espionage)
    Bibliography: p.
    Includes index.
    Summary: Provides a history of the Russian secret service, from the days of the czars to the present.
    1. Soviet Union. Komitet gosudarstvennoi bezopasnosti—History. 2. Secret service—Soviet Union—History. 3. Internal security—Soviet Union—History. 4.Political crimes and offenses—Soviet Union—Prevention—History. [1.KGB—History. 2. Secret service—Soviet Union—History. 3. Internal Security—Soviet Union—History] I. Title. II. Series: Yost, Graham. World espionage.
    HV8224.Y67 1989   363.3'83'0947   88-33396
    ISBN 0-8160-1940-1

British CIP data available on request

Facts On File books are available at special discounts when purchased in bulk quantities for businesses, associations, institutions, or sales promotion. Please contact the Special Sales department of our New York office at 212/683-2244 (dial 800/322-8755 except in NY, AK or HI).

Jacket design by Cathy Hyman
Composition by Facts On File, Inc.
Printed in the United States of America

10 9 8 7 6 5 4 3 2 1

This book is printed on acid-free paper.

CONTENTS

PREFACE

It would seem natural that a volume of the World Espionage series would be devoted to the KGB. The KGB, after all, is the Soviet spy agency, widely thought of as the Russian equivalent of America's spy agency, the CIA. As you read this book, however, you might be in for something of a surprise. This volume is not just a compendium of Russian spy stories. They are in here, but there is much more, for the KGB is much more than a spy agency.

Along with the stories of spy intrigue, you are going to find stories of political intrigue, of high-level power plays, and plots full of back-stabbing and double crosses. While the KGB does have spies around the world, it plays a far more important role inside the Soviet Union than that of merely gathering intelligence. As we will see, it is also responsible for internal security—squashing dissent, keeping the people in line. All told though, the KGB plays a role in the Soviet Union that is far greater than its spying and internal security functions combined. Nowhere is the old maxim "the whole is greater than the sum of its parts" truer than in the case of the KGB and the USSR.

We will see in this book how the KGB and its predecessors form one corner of a triad, made up of itself, the military, and the ruling communist party. This may be a surprise. We in the West hear about the doings of the communist party a fair amount, and every now and then we hear about the Russian army fighting in Afghanistan or Soviet military advisors in Nicaragua. Because the KGB is the *secret* police, we often don't hear about its activities. But it is powerful— some would say even more powerful than the other two corners of the triad. They would say that over the last 70 years the KGB has *been* the Soviet Union, that it has characterized the country and its government more than has communism or the military.

The KGB may be hard to see, but it has eyes and ears throughout the Soviet Union, at every level of government and society. And wherever the Soviet Union is around the world, the KGB is there, too, recruiting spies, infiltrating governments, gathering intelligence. The KGB was in Afghanistan before the Red Army tanks rolled in in 1979, and it will remain there after the tanks leave.

In many ways, this volume is the most important of the series, for it shows how intelligence gathering can affect a political system, especially when a spy agency gathers information on its country's own citizens.

This volume has extra importance because of what is going on in the Soviet Union at this time. Soviet leader Mikhail Gorbachev is attempting to institute reforms that will drastically alter the way his country works. Whether Gorbachev succeeds or not, the Soviet Union may never be the same, and along with it, the KGB. But, to understand what's going on, to understand what it means when Gorbachev puts his own man in as KGB chief, one has to understand what has been going on in the Soviet Union for the past 70 years, and a good way to understand that is to take a good look at the KGB and the tradition that precedes it.

INTRODUCTION

The Union of Soviet Socialist Republics—popularly, the Soviet Union—is the largest country, in land area, in the world, covering roughly 8.6 million square miles, or two-and-a-half times the area of the United States. This huge nation, which runs right across the top of the Eurasian landmass, from North Atlantic to North Pacific, is home to over 277,000,000 people, of various ethnic groups and nationalities.

The Soviet Union came into being in 1917 after the revolution in November of that year. The system of government is communist, based on the theories and writings of Karl Marx, a 19th-century social and political thinker and critic, who, along with his collaborator Friedrich Engels, conceived of a system of government and society where there would be no classes—no workers and bosses—and where everyone would share in the labor and in the rewards.

The communist revolution was led by Vladimir Ilyich Lenin, who headed a revolutionary group known as the Bolsheviks. Lenin added enough of his own input to Marxist theory so that, properly, the political theory guiding the Soviet state is Marxist-Leninism. Lenin's main input was the concept of a one-party state. That is, while in the United States there are two main political parties, the Republicans and the Democrats, in the USSR there is only one party, the communist party (the CPSU—Communist Party of the Soviet Union) running the whole country.

In theory, the country is run by elected officials. It is the *Soviet* Union because the government is composed of "soviets." A soviet is any council of elected officials, from the town level all the way up to the national level. The most powerful soviet is the one at the national level—the Supreme Soviet. Of course the election process is something of a mirage. The communist party puts forward its candidate, whether the election is for a local soviet or the Supreme Soviet, and, as there is no opposition allowed, the CPSU's candidate is automatically elected.

Nevertheless, according to theory, the Supreme Soviet is at the head of the country, given the power to make laws. The USSR's equivalent of the US president is supposedly the premier, who is the leader of the Supreme Soviet. The Supreme Soviet in turn appoints members to the Presidium, which operates the day- to-day high-level functioning of the government. The Supreme Soviet also elects the Council of Ministers, which—again, in theory—is the rough equivalent of the presidential cabinet in the US, composed of the various secretaries of departments, which, in the Soviet Union, are called ministries (Ministry of the Interior, Ministry of the Treasury, etc.).

In truth, the entire elected government—from the Supreme Soviet, Presidium, and Council of Ministers down to the local soviets—is subordinate to the party. The party, in turn, is governed by a ruling elite called the Politburo (short for Political Bureau). At the head of the Politburo is the true leader of the USSR, the general secretary of the communist party of the Soviet Union. The general secretary has, on occasion, also held the post of premier of the Supreme Soviet.

Although the revolution occurred in 1917, the Soviet Union didn't officially become the Union of Soviet Socialist Republics until 1923. From then on, as the name states, it became a union of theoretically independent republics. The largest of the republics is the Russian Soviet Federated Republic (RSFR), and it includes the European part of the country (with such cities as Moscow, Leningrad, and Kiev) and Siberia, the vast frozen land in the north and far east. It is usually the RSFR we are thinking of when we think of

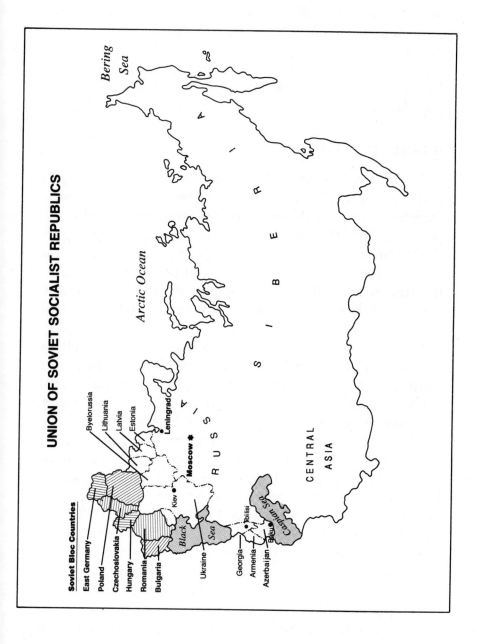

UNION OF SOVIET SOCIALIST REPUBLICS

Bering Sea

Arctic Ocean

SIBERIA

RUSSIA

CENTRAL ASIA

Leningrad

Moscow

Kiev

Byelorussia
Lithuania
Latvia
Estonia

Black Sea

Caspian Sea

Tbilisi

Baku

Soviet Bloc Countries
East Germany
Poland
Czechoslovakia
Hungary
Romania
Bulgaria

Ukraine

Georgia
Armenia
Azerbaijan

"Russia" as it corresponds to what Russia was in the 18th and 19th centuries. Although there are 14 other republics, including Latvia, Lithuania, the Ukraine, Armenia, Georgia, Turkmenistan, and Uzbekistan, and although they are supposed to be independent and share overall power, in truth the country is dominated by the RSFR. And, although ethnic Russians now only make up slightly less than half of the population, it is they who run the country.

A BRIEF HISTORY

Russia has been inhabited from 2000 BC on. The region takes its name from the Rus civilization that flourished in the eighth and ninth centuries AD. The realm of the Rus stretched from the Volga river south to the northern edge of the Byzantine empire. In the 10th century, Sviatoslav, the Prince of Kiev (one of the first major cities in the land) united the Rus and formed the first Russian state. His son, Vladimir, completed his father's work and brought Christianity to the forming nation.

The region was overrun by the Mongol hordes led by Genghis Khan in 1240. The land remained under Mongol control for over 200 years. At the beginning of that period the seat of power in the region was in the city of Novgorod. But over the years, the small city of Muscovy—Moscow—began its rise, and by the 14th century it had become the center of the land, and the rulers of the Russians were the Muscovite princes and grand princes. Thus began the Danilovich dynasty, named after the first Muscovite ruler, Prince Daniel, who ruled from 1276 to 1303. The Mongols were eventually routed from the land, in 1492, by Prince Ivan III, known as Ivan the Great.

The first czar of Russia was Ivan IV, known quite accurately to history as Ivan the Terrible for his ruthless eradication of all opposition in his quest for total power. The title czar was the Russian equivalent of caesar or emperor, and Ivan the Terrible—who took the title czar in 1547—was the first to forge a Russian empire. As we will see in chapter 1, he was also the first Russian leader to make use of a secret police, beginning a tradition that is expressed in the KGB of today.

Finding a successor to Ivan the Terrible was a problem. His son, Fyodor, was severely mentally handicapped, and although he took the title of czar, the country was actually ruled by the regent, Boris Godunov. When Godunov assumed the actual title of czar in 1598, the country entered what is now known as the Time of Troubles. There were five changes of leadership in the ensuing 15 years. The period of turbulence ended in 1613 when Michael Romanov was elected czar. Thus began the Romanov dynasty, which remained in power until 1917 (at least in name—although the Romanov bloodline ran out in 1761, succeeding royal families took the name Romanov).

The most notable of the Romanov czars was undoubtably Peter the Great, who ruled from 1682 to 1725. He sought to modernize and Westernize Russia, as well as expand the empire, making Russia a true European power. Peter attempted to make his country in a sense less Russian; French became the official language of the royal court and Peter called himself emperor, a European title, rather than the more Russian title czar (this makes Russian history confusing, with some leaders called czars, others emperors, and female sovereigns titled as both czarina and Empress). Empresses Elizabeth and Catherine the Great continued Peter's efforts to expand the empire, attaching the Crimea, the Ukraine, and much of Poland.

Czar Alexander I (1801-1825) attempted reforms, specifically concerning the system of serfdom in which peasants were essentially slaves to the aristocrats that owned the land they worked on. But he was sidetracked by the War of 1812, during which Russia battled Napoleon and the armies of France. His successor, Nicholas, was in no mood for reforms and ran Russia with an iron hand. It was during the time of Nicholas (1825-1855) that the first revolutionary undercurrents began to flow.

Nicholas's successor, Alexander II, did effect reforms and brought serfdom to an end. By that time, however, the revolutionary movement, aimed at overthrowing the czarist government, was gaining momentum, and Alexander II was assassinated by revolutionaries in 1881. In that year, the man who would later lead the revolution of 1917 was only 11 years old.

LENIN AND THE REVOLUTION

Vladimir Ilyich Lenin, the architect of the Soviet state, was born on April 22, 1870, in the town of Simbirsk. His real name was Vladimir Ilyich Ulyanov—he took the name Lenin in 1901 when he had to go undercover to avoid being captured by the czarist authorities.

Lenin's father was a teacher and by all accounts his family was a warm, happy one. That young Lenin would become involved with revolutionaries was not unusual for that time. Many young people fought against the injustices perpetrated by the czarist regime. But young Lenin was spurred on to become more of an activist and extremist when an older brother was arrested and executed for his alleged involvement in a plot against the life of Czar Alexander III.

In trying to plot the evolution of Lenin's revolutionary thought, it becomes apparent that even very early on his ideas tended towards a government with strict, central control by one group—the communist party.

This put Lenin in sharp disagreement with the leaders of the revolutionary movement at that time, the Mensheviks (roughly translated as "minoritarians," meaning people who represent the minority), who opposed any form of dictatorship and felt that a revolutionary government should be freely elected by the people. In response to the Mensheviks, Lenin called his relatively small splinter group the Bolsheviks ("majoritarians"— claiming to represent the majority). Despite the deep division between the Mensheviks and the Bolsheviks, the two groups did manage to

A picture of Lenin and his wife taken in the village of Gorki, November 1937. [Credit: UPI/Bettmann Newsphotos]

put their differences aside to work together for the common goal of revolution.

The first attempts at revolution began after Russia's loss in its war with Japan in the early part of the 20th century. Anger over the war, scarcity of food, and oppressive working conditions brought things to a boiling point. There were widespread riots and strikes, culminating in a massacre of protestors on January 22, 1905—known as Bloody Sunday. In the wake of this unrest, Czar Nicholas II formed Russia's first elected parliament, known as the Duma, in 1906. Several Dumas were held between 1906 and 1917.

World War I swept through Europe from the summer of 1914 on. Czar Nicholas entered Russia into the war. It was a disaster; by the fall of 1915 more than 1 million Russian soldiers had been killed. Tremendous unrest stirred in the land and in March 1917 Czar Nicholas II was deposed (later killed) and the Romanov dynasty came to an end. A democratic, provisional government, assembled by Aleksandr Kerensky, came to power. The Kerensky government was supported by many of the moderate, more Menshevik soviets (workers' councils). Many, such as Leon Trotsky—a leading Menshevik thinker—hailed the provisional government as a good first step toward true revolution.

Lenin, however, was not so pleased. He returned from self-imposed exile in Switzerland to denounce the provisional government as liberal and bourgeois (that is, middle-class). But Lenin's was still a small voice at that time and the Bolsheviks carried little weight.

The Bolsheviks gained in credibility and influence when the provisional government cracked down on them in the summer of 1917. This action turned several angry Mensheviks—including Trotsky—into Bolsheviks. As well, many of the promises of the Kerensky government—more bread, ending the war with Germany—were going unfulfilled. Lenin, who had again gone into exile (in Finland this time), urged armed revolution from abroad. Despite unrest, Lenin's calls went unheeded. So, on October 23, he snuck into Petrograd, and, in a 10-hour debate with his fellow Bolsheviks, convinced them that now was the time for all-out revolution. The final plans for the military move were put in the hands of Trotsky. On November 7 and 8, armed members of soldiers' and sailors' soviets overthrew the provisional government.

For the most part, it was a bloodless revolution. The blood really began to flow in the following years during the civil war, as Lenin and the Bolsheviks sought to secure their power against the challenges of the Mensheviks, other rival revolutionaries, the White Russians (the Kerensky supporters), and czarists. The civil war ended in 1920.

In the last years of his life, Lenin found himself caught between the more totalitarian members of the CPSU, such as Josef Stalin, who wanted the country to be run under very strict central control, and the more moderate, democratically minded, such as Trotsky. We will cover this struggle more closely in a later chapter, as its outcome—the rise of Stalin—set the tone for the ensuing 60 years of Soviet history.

And what does all of this have to do with the KGB? If it wasn't for the early precursor of the KGB, Lenin would not have succeeded and the Soviet state would not have survived.

THE SWORD AND SHIELD

The reason Lenin and his colleagues were able to gain power and hold onto it was because of the success of the Red Army—the creation of Trotsky, which overcame all military resistance—and because of the success of the Cheka, the secret police, which, under the guidance of Felix Dzerzhinsky, ferreted out and exterminated all political resistance through wave after wave of mass terror.

According to Marxist-Leninist doctrine, the Cheka should have become unnecessary after the resistance—the "counter-revolution"—was suppressed, but Lenin and his successors realized that their war would be an unending one. To maintain totalitarian control over such a huge and diverse populace required the use of such a tool as the Cheka on an ongoing basis. The leaders realized that the "dictatorship of the proletariat" (*proletariat* is a marxist term for the working class) was vulnerable to the very thing that had put it in power in the first place—popular unrest. This meant that the communist party was equally vulnerable. And so, a Cheka would always be needed, as "the sword and shield" of the revolution and the party.

The name of the secret police has changed perhaps a dozen times between then and now. Today it is the KGB, . and has been called this for over 30 years. Because there have been so many name changes over the years, some just call the Russian secret police "the organs"—as in "the organs of state security." One of the most interesting things about "the organs," as we will see, is that they didn't begin with the Soviet state. On the contrary, their lineage can be traced back farther than that— back 700 years to the time of the Mongol conqueror and tyrant Genghis Khan.

The KGB has a place in Russian history at the end of a long succession of secret services that stretches back for centuries. It is not just a creation of the present Soviet government of Russia—it is, to some extent, a creation of the whole history of Russia. The organs, the secret police, are something of a Russian tradition.

1.

FROM THE OPRICHNIKI TO THE OCHRANA

Genghis Khan was a short, ugly man with a clubfoot. He was also one of the most formidable military conquerors the world has ever known. He stormed out of the steppes of Mongolia with his hordes in the 13th century and swept across Asia and into Russia, conquering and subjugating whole peoples and nations as he went. His awesome success did not rest on superior numbers or technology; indeed, on occasion, he defeated forces larger and better armed than his. One of the crucial factors in his campaign across Asia was intelligence. Not so much his own intelligence—although he was undoubtedly a brilliant military tactician— but the intelligence he had his spies collect.

Centuries before Genghis Khan, Sun Tzu, a Chinese philosopher, in his treatise, "The Art of War," exalted the value of spying, seeing it as one of the keys to victory. Genghis Khan's innovation was to send men on ahead of his advancing hordes, having them pose as deserters fleeing the khan (a tactic KGB chief Yuri Andropov would use some 700 years later when he placed spies among those fleeing the Soviet invasion of Hungary in 1956). Once they had scouted the terrain and the forces preparing to fight the Mongols, the spies would slip back to rejoin the khan and tell what they had discovered. Armed with this vital information, Genghis Khan inevitably prevailed in the ensuing battles.

The Mongol occupying force maintained control of Russia for over 200 years, but Genghis Khan's descendants could not hold the land forever. In 1492, Russian hero Ivan the

11

Great, having marshalled the various factions in Russia, expelled the occupying Mongol armies. But, as the hordes retreated back across the mountains and plains of Central Asia, not all traces of Genghis Khan went with them. One legacy of his remained: his successors discovered that spies were useful, not only during wartime but also during times of quiet, especially when trying to subdue a people against their will. Even then, 500 years ago, the leader of Russia saw such an apparatus as the key to power and survival.

THE OPRICHNIKI

In the 1500s, Czar Ivan IV—aptly known to history as Ivan the Terrible—became the first Russian leader to give his secret police a name, the *Oprichniki*. The name is derived from the rather innocent word *oprichnina*, which is what estates given to widowed princesses were called. Ivan's secret police received the odd name rather circuitously.

Ivan's plan was to destroy the *boyars*, the feudal aristocracy in power in Russia at the time. His first step was to establish his own separate state within the czardom, which he quaintly called his "oprichnina." Hence, his secret police force became know as the Oprichniki. Using his oprichnina as a starting point, and using the Oprichniki as an instrument of terror and coercion, Ivan brought down the boyars.

As in the KGB today, the Oprichniki were sworn to complete secrecy and loyalty to the czar. In return, they were rewarded greatly. They were given the estates of the deposed boyars. A palace and whole section of Moscow became theirs. They were unaccountable to anyone but the czar. And there was the gruesome perk attached to the job: dressed in black and riding black horses, the Oprichniki had license to kill anyone they pleased. In one five-week period in the city of Novgorod, the Oprichniki massacred 60,000 citizens, employing horrifying means of torture and execution, including the drowning of thousands of women and children in the city's river.

Eventually, even for Czar Ivan, the Oprichniki went too far. Not because of their heinous crimes, mind you, but because they were becoming too formidable a power unto themselves. And so, he dismembered his monster.

But the monster never really died. It went on living under a different name. The idea of a secret police force proved too enticing to those in power to resist. The organs became a fixture. Under the Romanovs they became a bureaucracy. In the 1600s Czar Michael Romanov created the Tainy Prikaz— the Bureau of Secret Affairs. Later, in 1704, Czar Peter the Great called his secret police the Special Office of the Czar.

With Empress Catherine II, the organs gained the rather mysterious and romantic name The Secret Expedition. Catherine's successor at the Russian court was her son, Paul, who became czar in 1796. He is remembered as a foolish and cruel man. Paul would have anyone exiled or executed under the slightest pretext.

Paul didn't last long in the job. His son, Alexander, conspired with a group of disgruntled army officers to have his father murdered in his sleep. For his day, Alexander was something of a liberal and on April 1, 1801, he abolished the Secret Expedition.

Good intentions he may have had, but it wasn't long before Alexander set up his own secret service. While up until then the Russian secret police forces had been working internally, squashing dissent and opposition, under Alexander it was in foreign espionage that his spies really made their mark. Their first big coup was to send a spy team to Paris, headed by a young colonel named Tchernikov, who managed to obtain Napoleon's plans for the invasion of Russia. During Russia's war with France, the ace spy for the Russians was a Colonel Figuer, a master of disguises and accents who would slip back and forth across the battle lines. On one occasion he convinced the commandant of French troops in Danzig that he was a French officer. He was wined and dined and given highly classified messages to deliver to Napoleon—which he, of course, delivered to the Russian generals instead.

Alexander died in 1825 and was succeeded as czar by his second brother, Nicholas. Czar Nicholas's reign was a stark contrast to the almost liberal regime of his brother. He revamped the secret service and created the Third Section of His Majesty's Private Imperial Chancery.

The Third Section was a true 1800s version of the KGB. Indeed Nicholas came up with some innovations that have been popular tools of the organs in Russia ever since. He was the first to use Siberia as a place to which dissidents could be banished. He also had the Third Section infiltrate the ranks of disgruntled émigrés (people who fled Nicholas's oppression to live in other countries), something which the KGB does to this day.

The reign of suspicion and terror passed when Nicholas did. In 1855, he was succeeded by Czar Alexander II. Like the Alexander before him, Alexander II was a liberal, and he did his best to right the wrongs of Nicholas's regime. He put the Third Section on a short leash and drastically reduced its powers. Eventually, he abolished it altogether.

But a pattern had been established by this time, one that resisted change. For, while it may have been Czar Alexander II's wish to rid the state of a secret police force, nonetheless he eventually created his own. Perhaps he didn't think of it as a secret force, but that's what it was. It was the Department of State Protection—the Okrannoye Otdyelyenye, known simply as the Ochrana.

THE OCHRANA

Russia, in the latter half of the 19th century, was a hotbed of revolutionary thought. Even a "liberal" czar such as Alexander was still a dictator. The people in general were very poor and oppressed, with little say in how their lives were governed. There were many different revolutionary groups. They began plotting, together and separately, to bring down the czars through violent means, including bombings and assassinations.

On Sunday, March 1, 1881, Czar Alexander II's horse-drawn sledge passed by a cheese factory on a side street. The first bomb thrown killed the Czar's two guards. When Alexander went to try to help the men, a second bomb killed him.

Alexander had abolished the Third Section, the secret police of his predecessor, Czar Nicholas, because it was an affront to his liberal sensibilities. The Ochrana, which he created to take the Third Section's place started small. After his death, however, it grew rapidly and quickly became huge.

Once again the Russians had a mind-bogglingly comprehensive and all-pervasive internal security service. The Ochrana was everywhere, its agents spying on everyone. There were agents watching every train station; agents disguised as bellhops in every hotel; agents working as ushers in theaters; agents just walking the streets keeping their eyes and ears open. All mail was opened and read. There was even a 24-hour store in St. Petersburg that was used to supply agents with disguises at all hours.

The technique the Ochrana used most often in its effort to break up the revolutionaries was a rather devious and questionable one—the agent provocateur.

THE PROVOCATEURS

The term *agent provocateur* is taken from the French; it means an agent who provokes. Such an agent is used not only to infiltrate and spy on a group but to actually provoke the group into committing a criminal action.

In a typical operation, the Ochrana used a female student to infiltrate a group called the Revolutionary Socialists. Once accepted in the group she suggested a plan to assassinate the governor of Minsk. The Ochrana let her go through with the assassination attempt, although with a bomb they had diffused. This brought members of the Revolutionary Socialists into the open where they could be arrested.

Legally, using provocateurs is an unethical method. Unprovoked, the group infiltrated might not do anything illegal. Legality, however, was not a major concern of the Ochrana. Its biggest concern was whether or not using provocateurs was effective.

Many of the people used as provocateurs were "turned" revolutionaries; some were even criminals. Could they be trusted? At best, running provocateur operations was a murky business, and the best example of how murky it could get was the scandalous case of Ievno Azeff.

Ievno Azeff was born in 1869. In the early 1890s, as a student, he was a member of a revolutionary group. In 1892, when he was about to be arrested, he fled to Geneva. He entered the Polytechnic Institute and hooked up with other Russian radicals living in exile, in particular the Russian Social Democratic Group. Then, of his own accord, he decided to betray his cohorts as a way to make money. He wrote to the police suggesting this, and the Ochrana eventually contacted him. They were hesitant about using him as a provocateur—afraid that he was trying to trick them—but finally signed him on in June 1893. He repaid their trust quickly and well, by betraying people and plans and by provoking the young revolutionaries into acts of violence.

Azeff did so well that he was recalled to Moscow to continue his work there. Azeff supplied the Ochrana with the desired information on the Moscow revolutionary groups—leaders' names, plans, etc. At the same time he didn't remain just another revolutionary himself but began to rise rapidly in the ranks. He rose high enough to get access to what was called the "Battle Organization"—the radicals' name for their master plan of assassinations and violence.

However, while he told the Ochrana much of the Battle Organization, he didn't give away the man at the top of the plan, G. A. Gershuni. He betrayed Gershuni's subordinates, but never the leader himself. Azeff even went so far as to tell the Ochrana expressly not to arrest Gershuni, and this, as it turned out, was shortly before Gershuni arranged for the assassination of the minister of the interior. Azeff did finally reveal Gershuni's identity, but not until Gershuni had fled the country.

In retrospect it seems apparent that Azeff was working for both sides, but at that time neither side caught on. He continued to rise within the revolutionary scene, advocating ever more violence while at the same time betraying many of those around him. In fact, he used his connection with the Ochrana to facilitate his rise among the radicals. If anyone stood in his way among the revolutionaries, he'd simply turn that person in.

Ironically, Azeff was almost caught at this time, not by the Ochrana, however, but by the revolutionaries. By this time, the revolutionaries had begun to place radical agents within the Ochrana. One of these found evidence of Azeff's duplicity and reported it to the Social Revolution Committee, stating that "Azeff is betraying the party." However, by that point Azeff had reached such prominence in the movement that the man was ignored.

There was, however, someone else on the trail of Azeff. He was V. L. Burtsev, a journalist and editor who supported the revolutionaries. He knew someone from within the movement was betraying it, but he didn't know who—until he hooked up with a revolutionary leader by the name of Lapuchin. All Burtsev had on the traitor was the code name the Ochrana used for him. Lapuchin had once been chief of police and he knew what the code name stood for—it stood for Ievno Azeff.

Burtsev then published his accusation, but he left Lapuchin—at Lapuchin's request—out of it. Again, Azeff's popularity and power within the movement came to his rescue. Not only did no one believe Burtsev's accusations, they actually put him on a kind of trial for libel. One of the judges said Burtsev should shoot himself for the damage he'd caused to the revolution. His back up against the wall,

Burtsev told how he'd obtained his confirmation through Lapuchin.

Now the tide turned against Azeff. But still he wasn't finished. He quickly set in motion a plan to assassinate the czar to prove his allegiance to the revolution—but the plan fizzled. Revolutionary agents tracked Azeff down in Paris to question him. But, instead of killing him immediately, they gave him one more night—they still couldn't believe that Comrade Azeff was a traitor! Azeff used the extra night to flee France with his mistress. After that his trail became hard to follow and the revolutionaries never did catch up with him. It is believed that he died in Germany in 1918. Chances are no one will ever truly know which side Azeff really was working for or which side he betrayed the most.

Azeff was only one of many provocateurs that the Ochrana used. Some were not as successful in playing the part as was Azeff. A priest by the name of Gapon who was part of the revolutionary movement agreed to be a provocateur for the Ochrana when he was down on his luck. The revolutionaries discovered his betrayal and hung him from a rafter with clothesline.

Many of the provocateur operations were carried out abroad. The East End of London was a prime gathering spot for Russian revolutionaries who had fled their homeland and were laying low for a while. Knowing this, the Ochrana sent in a large number of provocateurs to stir things up and get the revolutionaries into trouble with the British authorities. Some believe that one wild incident, the Sidney Street Siege of 1910, wherein British police fought a gang of Russian revolutionaries, in the end burning down their house, was actually a provocation of the Ochrana. Perhaps the wildest theory though, is that the infamous Jack the Ripper—an unknown killer who murdered six prostitutes in London's East End—was actually an Ochrana provocateur, a criminally insane surgeon who went by the name Mikhail Ostrog.

The problem with all provocateur operations, as illustrated most pointedly by the Azeff affair, was the question of trust. The first head of the Ochrana, from 1866 to 1874, was Count P. A. Schuvaloff. In "A History of the Russian Secret Service" author Richard Deacon notes that when Schuvaloff later became ambassador to England, he watched the provocateurs at work and became critical of their actions, writing:

> There is no end to this game of spies. From what I see here in London you set the criminal exiles to spy on the Radicals and then, to be quite sure, you need to find spies to watch the criminals, and it has even happened that a criminal is spying on the very Radical who has been selected by one of my attaches to spy on the criminal. I do not say this is but an exception, but the fact that it happens at all is surely an indication of how such madness can spread.

But provocateurs weren't the only agents the Ochrana used. It also employed good old fashioned spies.

SIDNEY REILLY

The early years of Sidney Reilly are a little hazy. According to one story, Reilly was born in Russia on March 24, 1874, near the city of Odessa. About the only thing that is known for sure is that Sidney Reilly was not his real name. His true name is believed to have been Sigmund Georgievich Rosenblum. Legend has it that his parents were Polish Jews and that as a young man he rebelled against his family and fled to South America. It was there, the story goes, that he met a British secret service agent and saved his life. As a reward for his heroics, the British agent gave Reilly a trip to Britain and a meeting with the secret service. Reilly, with his new name, was hired by the British and began his career as a spy.

It wasn't long before Reilly became what is known as a double agent—working for two countries at once. In particular Reilly found himself both spying *on* and spying *for* Russia.

There is one, perhaps fictional, story about Reilly. It is said that when he was working for the Ochrana he had a run- in with a fellow agent he felt, like Azeff, was doing more to help the revolutionaries than to hurt them. The name of the man was Josef Vissarionvich Dzhugashvili—the real name of Josef Stalin, who ruled the Soviet Union from 1924 to 1953, and was arguably the most ruthless and murderous tyrant Russia has ever known. According to this story, when Reilly voiced his objections about young Josef to the Ochrana they defended him, saying that he gave them good information. Reilly pointed out to them that the information didn't concern Josef's friends, the Bolsheviks, but only betrayed the Mensheviks, a rival revolutionary group.

In the years leading up to World War I, Reilly expanded his repertoire. He became a triple agent, working, at various times, for Britain, Russia, and Germany. With his charm and grace he moved easily in the highest circles. In many ways he was the real-life version of James Bond, cutting a dashing figure in a tuxedo. But he was also a ruthless, brutal man, known to kill people to keep them quiet or if they got in the way of his plans.

No one has ever been quite sure who benefited most from Reilly's exploits—besides Reilly himself, of course. In the years leading up to World War I, Reilly did his best work for the Russians, obtaining vital information on German aircraft and naval design. When the war came, Reilly dropped out of sight as far as Russia was concerned. The next time he appeared in Russia was years later, after it had become the Soviet Union.

WORLD WAR I

Although dashing, Reilly wasn't the most important Russian agent in the years before the war. That honor fell to Colonel Alfred Redl of Austria, who, to say the least, was a reluctant spy. Redl was the chief of counterintelligence in Austria. The Russians discovered that he was a homosexual. If that fact had come out then it would have destroyed his life. So when the Russians threatened to expose Redl's sexual orientation, he had little choice but to do as they asked.

What the Russians received from Redl was awesome. He gave them a list of every Austrian spy at work in Russia. He also gave them a copy of the Austrian battle plan to invade Russia if and when war broke out. Redl went so far as to secretly photograph and fingerprint every agent who came into his office—and, as head of counterintelligence, he had the authority to bring every agent into his office at one time or another—and then sent this intelligence to Russia. He also betrayed the highest level codes used by the Austrians.

Redl's end as a spy came in 1913. He had been suspected of espionage as early as 1912, but there had been no proof. Investigators were stymied. Then, post office censors opened some letters posted from a town near the Russian border. The letters were filled with money. Suspicious, they put a watch on to see who picked up the letters. It was Redl. Still, no one could quite believe it. So, Redl was followed secretly for a time. Redl knew he was being tailed and, panicking, he made a bad blunder for a spy. He was carrying some incriminating evidence, material that would connect him to known Russian spies. Instead of burning the paper, or chewing and swallowing it, he tore it up and threw if away. The agents following him retrieved it, pasted it back together, and they had their proof. Agents were sent to confront Redl. He knew what was expected of him. The agents gave Redl a pistol; he went to his room and shot himself, leaving a note asking for their prayers.

The intelligence Russia received from Redl—everything from plans of army installations to maps and cipher books—is said to have accounted for many Russian victories over Austria early in the war.

During the war, the Russians were fanatically anti- German, and the Ochrana reflected this. One man was sent to Siberia simply because he'd lived in Germany for two years. Another was arrested when he was spotted on a St. Petersburg street with his collar turned up, because there was a rumor circulating that German agents in St. Petersburg were walking around with their collars turned up.

But the Ochrana wasn't just looking for German agents during the war. It still had the ongoing struggle with the revolutionaries to contend with, and it was losing the battle. The revolutionaries took advantage of the instability created by the war and continued to grow. The war was a disaster for Russia and the people were very unhappy. It was a country ripe for revolution. And, in the end, the Ochrana itself was so thoroughly infiltrated with revolutionary agents that it became almost useless.

As we have seen, when the czarist government collapsed, the provisional government that took over couldn't hold on to power. The revolutionary momentum was unstoppable by this time.

The Revolution of 1917 marked the end of Russia as it had been for centuries and the beginning of the Soviet Union. That fall of 1917 also marked the end of the Ochrana—and the beginning of a new secret police.

2.

THE CHEKA

Lenin's great accomplishment was not the revolution so much as how he managed to maneuver the Bolsheviks into a position of supremacy. It was not an easy battle. It took several years and cost millions of lives. In fact, it was such a terrible ordeal that whatever Lenin's dreams and goals for his country had been before the revolution, by the time the Bolsheviks were firmly in control of the country, the character of the Soviet Union was set for the next 70 years, and the character was not one of "workers' paradise," but of ruthless tyranny.

Lenin did not manage the feat alone. Indeed, his forceful leadership notwithstanding, Bolshevik control of the government was largely the result of the efforts of two other men. One was Leon Trotsky, a bookish-looking little man who almost singlehandedly created the Red Army, the military force that the Bolsheviks used to crush their opposition. The other man was the head of the secret police.

Lenin knew that while Trotsky and the Red Army would fight the military battles, the Bolsheviks would also need a tool to use against political opponents—the czarists, the White Russians loyal to the Kerensky government and, most importantly, the rival revolutionaries. To fight this fight he would need a secret police force not unlike the hated Ochrana that had just been dismembered.

On December 20, 1917, the Extraordinary Commission to Combat Counterrevolution and Sabotage was created. Its Russian name was Chrevzuchaynaya Komissiya po Borbe s Kontrarevolutisyei i Sabotazhem. This rather lengthy name

23

was soon shortened to a four-letter acronym, vChK, and simply called the "Cheka." The man Lenin chose to head his secret police was Felix Edmundovich Dzerzhinsky.

FELIX DZERZHINSKY

Felix Dzerzhinsky was born on September 11, 1877, in Vilna, Lithuania, to an aristocratic Polish family with considerable land holdings. His father was a professor.

Dzerzhinsky did reasonably well in school (although he failed Russian and had to take a course in the language a second time) and was particularly interested in logic and politics. He was raised a Roman Catholic and for a time considered entering the priesthood. He never did, for at the age of 18 he joined the local Lithuanian Social Democratic Party and had his first introduction to the writings of Karl Marx. Then, when the Ochrana executed his younger brother for having written poetry that supported the idea of a revolution, Dzerzhinsky was pushed further into the revolutionary movement.

In the autumn of 1896 Dzerzhinsky moved to Moscow, where he enrolled at the university. It wasn't long before he had hooked up with some underground political groups. After he instigated a couple of assaults on the Ochrana, Dzerzhinsky was arrested for crimes against the state and sent to Siberia with a five-year sentence. He was 19 years old.

In prison, Dzerzhinsky became a leader, not so much because of what he said but because of what he did. Dzerzhinsky's ability to withstand all the torture and punishment the Ochrana brought to bear on him impressed, even inspired, his fellow prisoners. He gained their respect to such an extent that on August 28, 1899, they helped him escape.

Dzerzhinsky's freedom was short-lived. He was turned in by an Ochrana informer in January 1900 and sent back to prison. The bonds and loyalties he made while in prison

Felix Dzerzhinsky, founder of the Cheka, precursor of the KGB. [Credit: UPI/Bettmann Newsphotos]

served him all his life—many of the men he hired later as agents of the Cheka were people he met in prison.

Dzerzhinsky escaped again, in 1902. This time he stayed free for much longer. In 1906, at a Bolshevik conclave in Stockholm, he met Lenin and Stalin, who were both impressed with young Felix; his scars from prison and his status as an escapee showed his dedication to the revolution.

In November 1910, Dzerzhinsky married fellow revolutionary Sofia Sigizmundovna Mushkat, while she was in Poland on a secret assignment for the movement. Neither Dzerzhinsky nor his wife stayed out of prison long. Sofia gave birth to Felix's son, Ian, in a women's prison in Warsaw in 1911. Dzerzhinsky saw his son briefly before being arrested in 1912.

This time Dzerzhinsky was sent to a prison camp in a copper mine in the Ural mountains and then, in 1916 was transferred to Butyrka, a notorious prison in Moscow where the most hardened criminals were held. He was sent to Butyrka because of a deteriorating case of tuberculosis (a progressive, and at that time often fatal, lung infection) and because officials in the Urals feared Dzerzhinsky would organize an uprising among the copper miners if he were to stay there.

In February and March 1917, after the fall of the Czarist regime, the short-lived provisional government released all political prisoners, including Dzerzhinsky. From then on he worked closely with Lenin to bring about the revolution.

Dzerzhinsky was by all accounts a quiet, slight, unassuming man. Only his eyes, steely blue, hinted at the fierceness in his soul, and only the scars on his arms, which he casually but proudly displayed, showed the horrors he had endured. He was shrewd, a brilliant organizer, and a genius at exploiting opportunities and the weaknesses of others. Everything he did as head of the Cheka was aimed at one thing—getting the Bolsheviks into power and keeping them there.

Although his first loyalty was to the party and the revolution, he was also reportedly a devoted husband and father. He was also supposedly quite compassionate. Indeed, some remember that tears would come to his eyes when he put his signature on yet another death warrant. In time, over a period of only a few years, those death warrants and the other forms of systematic annihilation of opposition— enacted not only by Dzerzhinsky but by Lenin, Trotsky, and the other architects of the revolution and the Bolshevik rise to power—would claim untold millions of Russian lives.

THE TERROR

"To save the revolution we must first destroy the counter-revolutionaries," said Dzerzhinsky (quoted in *The New KGB* by William R. Corson and Robert T. Crowley), at a reception he held in late December 1917 to celebrate the formation of the Cheka. The ramifications of those three words— "destroy the counterrevolutionaries"—are still being felt in the Soviet Union to this day.

The Cheka started small. Initially all Dzerzhinsky had was a staff of 23, including a teenage secretary. But it expanded quickly in its first year. Dzerzhinsky coerced the czar's legion of guards into being the first troops of the Cheka. He also moved the headquarters from Petrograd to Moscow. Within the year Dzerzhinsky had Chekists all across Russia, and in every town within a couple of years.

The Cheka's expansion was so rapid partly because Dzerzhinsky operated the Cheka completely extralegally; there were no laws or statutes governing the operation. Because of the unlimited powers there were abuses from the very beginning. But Dzerzhinsky could get away with it at first, ascribing the excesses to the overexuberance of young men devoted to the revolution. But he couldn't write it all off to the doings of "rogue Chekists" forever. In the summer of 1918, however, like a gift from heaven, Dzerzhinsky was given the excuse, indeed the mandate, to do with the Cheka as he saw fit. On August 30, 1918, Fania Kaplan, a Social Revolutionary party member—the Social Revolutionaries were communists, but rivals of the Bolsheviks— confronted Lenin as he left a meeting in Moscow, pulled out a gun, and shot him. Although the wounds were serious, Lenin survived the incident (Fania Kaplan did not—she was executed within the week).

The assassination attempt was all Dzerzhinsky needed to really set his Chekist thugs loose. It was then that "the terror" was unleashed. Tens of thousands of people were shot by the Cheka within days. The tide of blood did not subside for years.

That period, from 1917 to 1920, was a civil war of sorts, during which the Bolsheviks crushed their opposition and solidified their control. It is not called "the terror" simply because Western observers called it that. Terror was a term Lenin himself used quite a bit. According to *The New KGB* by Corson & Crowley, in January 1918 Lenin said, "We can achieve nothing unless we use terror." A few months later he said, "Terror is a direct necessity."

To give an idea of just what "the terror" meant, there is another quote, also from *The New KGB*, by N. V. Krylenko, who was at that time the public prosecutor of many of the cases the Chekists bothered to bring before the courts and who later became the minister of justice: "We must execute not only the guilty. Execution of the innocent will impress the masses even more."

Anyone who posed any threat at all, even if imagined, was sure to be shot. The first to go were the liberals and intellectuals—many of whom had supported the revolutionary movement—as well as virtually anyone who had worked for the previous government and leaders of the military. Just being a successful merchant was reason enough to warrant one's death.

By one estimate, the terror claimed the lives—through shootings, forced starvation, and deaths in prison and labor camps—of perhaps 20 million Russians. The scope of this terror is impossible to comprehend. As Stalin said, perhaps cynically, "One man's death is a tragedy; 10,000 deaths is merely a statistic." (Source: *The New KGB*.) And the deaths were not all swift. Torture was used.

The object was to create a climate of fear and dread where no one could feel safe; where everyone would be suspicious and afraid. Dzerzhinsky encouraged everyone to spy on everyone else. All trust was destroyed. Indeed, the only way to survive was to accuse others. Children were encouraged to inform on their parents. No one was above the Cheka's suspicion. Even the Bolshevik leaders had agents assigned to them and were the subject of surveillance and scrutiny.

Dzerzhinsky was also concerned about the Red Army's loyalty to the revolution. Trotsky had done amazing things in forming a fighting force during the upheaval of the revolution and its aftermath. In fact, for the tastes of Lenin and Dzerzhinsky he almost did too good a job. Lenin began to fear the power of the Red Army. So, he and Dzerzhinsky created the Cheka's Special Department—the Osobye Otdel—in February 1919.

The job of the OOs, as Special Department operatives became known, was to watch the Red Army and make sure that all officers and conscripts adhered to the correct political ideology and weren't secret counterrevolutionaries. The OOs went beyond that, of course, and they were brutal. They went with the Army wherever it went. The OOs would force troops into battle. If anyone lagged behind, the OOs would shoot them on the spot.

While today's descendants of the OOs aren't quite so ruthless and don't have nearly the unlimited powers of their ancestors, they are still called upon to keep the military in line politically. Even more than in other nations, the leaders of the Soviet Union have always been afraid of their military achieving too much independence.

One of Dzerzhinsky's first orders of business had been to isolate the political opponents by seizing control of all telephone and telegraph communications—if the "counterrevolutionaries" couldn't talk to each other, they couldn't organize. As the Chekist terror grew and expanded, Dzerzhinsky attempted to isolate each individual citizen. This was "population control." The Cheka began issuing ID—identification papers. People couldn't move around without this ID; therefore the Cheka was able to control everyone's movement. Of course to even get the ID in the first place people had to go to the Cheka to apply for it. In that way the whole ID procedure became another way for the Cheka to scrutinize the citizenry and pluck out any political undesirables.

Dzerzhinsky also created the Frontier Cheka, now known as the Border Guards. The duty of the Border Guards—who now have their own army, navy and air force—is to keep people in the Soviet Union, not keep them out. In those early days, most people caught by the Frontier Cheka trying to escape the country were either just shot or sent off to a prison or labor camp (where they would usually die in any event).

The Cheka was obsessed with all opposition to the revolution and the Bolsheviks, both inside and outside of the Soviet Union. The part of the Cheka that ran the domestic operations against the counterrevolutionaries was called the Counterespionage Section—the KRO (Kontrarazvedyvatelnyi Otdel). The operation of the KRO reflected Dzerzhinsky's growing ambitions for the Cheka. At first, the KRO worked against Soviet citizens. Then, Dzerzhinsky expanded its responsibilities to include spying on foreign citizens in the Soviet Union. It was then that the Cheka began to place its agents among the staffs of the various foreign embassies in Moscow (embassies usually employ locals to work in service positions—maid, cook, driver, etc.), a practice continued by the KGB to this day.

Dzerzhinsky then began to expand the reach of the Cheka even further. He wasn't satisfied with only disrupting opposition groups at home; he wanted to wreck them abroad as well. Many of the czarists and White Russians, the supporters of the Kerensky government, fled the country after the revolution. They were known as émigrés. They would gather together in foreign lands, some of them organizing and planning for the day when they could return to Russia and overthrow the Bolsheviks. Naturally, this wasn't appreciated by Dzerzhinsky.

THE FIRST SOVIET SPIES

Dzerzhinsky sent his Chekists to infiltrate the émigré groups. The goal wasn't merely to keep tabs on the groups, but to somehow lure the émigrés back to the Soviet Union so they could be executed. To do this, Dzerzhinsky used provocateurs. His agents would flee Russia as if they were anti-Bolsheviks and join the White Russian and czarist émigré groups in London, Paris, Geneva, etc. The agents would then be able to report home to Moscow on the activities of the groups, and if possible, arrange for émigrés to return home to certain death. Of course this was exactly the same technique the Ochrana had used in the years before the revolution when it infiltrated revolutionary groups abroad with its own provocateurs. Dzerzhinsky had learned well from his enemy.

Dzerzhinsky needed an apparatus to oversee this foreign espionage activity. On December 20, 1920, he created the Foreign Department—the INO (Inostrannyi Otdel)—to handle foreign operations. Initially, the INO was only concerned with émigré groups, but eventually it expanded its range and began spying on the governments of other nations.

The agents of the INO were the first Chekist spies. Initially they were classic loner spies—"singletons"—working all alone, undercover, in foreign capitals. After the civil war came to a close, Lenin began setting up Soviet embassies around the world, and Dzerzhinsky began stocking the staffs of these new embassies with INO agents. These agents were known as the "legals," for they were working under official cover at the embassies. The head INO agent in an embassy was the "legal resident" and usually held a position of first or second secretary or attaché. The INO legal resident—as with KGB legal residents to this day—in truth had much more power than the ambassador.

For some time after the revolution, however, while Lenin tried to set up embassies around the world, not every country—including the United States and Britain—was immediately receptive to establishing diplomatic relations. They balked at being friendly with a communist country that had as one of its stated aims the overthrow of the governments of these very capitalist nations. *But,* these capitalist nations were, at the same time, quite willing to do business with the communists.

The most famous of the Soviet trading organizations were Amtorg and Arcos. Amtorg—short for AMerican Trading ORGanization—was established in the United States in 1924. One of the founders was Armand Hammer, the American industrialist who has made a fortune from American-Soviet trade over the years, especially in the area of oil. Arcos—the All-Russian Cooperative Society—was the Soviet trading organization in London during the twenties. Little did the American and British businessmen who entered into agreements with these organizations know, blinded as they were by visions of vast untapped markets, that the Soviet commercial stations were set up for spying first and trade second.

In some instances—as these overeager businessmen would find out to their chagrin—trading wasn't even a consideration. A Soviet trading organization would make an order for, let's say, farm equipment, from an American manufacturer. The equipment would be shipped, but the manufacturer would never see a cent in payment and would have little recourse for recovery, as his country didn't have diplomatic relations with the Soviet Union.

Spies soon popped up around the globe in these commercial stations of the Cheka. Proof that this is what the trading organizations were up to was found in London in 1927. British security forces had uncovered a Soviet operative. They watched him receive stolen documents and tailed him back to Arcos, the Soviet's British trading organization. When they moved in to raid the premises they found their entry barred by a heavy steel door. It took them five hours to cut the bolts and get through the door. When finally they got through they found the place filled with smoke and the Soviets inside nearly dead from asphyxiation—they had followed instructions and had been burning all incriminating documents.

The Arcos trade representatives were arrested as spies and Arcos was shut down. Some of the spies defected and remained in England rather than return home to the harsh punishment that the organs promised for all who failed. Britain, of course, immediately suspended all relations with the Soviets. These relations were restored a few years later, however, and one of the primary reasons they were restored was the ever-alluring prospect of trade with the Soviets. All this quite strongly echoes the comment Lenin once made that capitalists will end up selling the revolutionaries the rope they will use to hang the capitalists.

Still, as important a development as the system of legal agents—through the embassies and trading organizations—was for the Cheka, it was the "illegals," the agents who operated undercover, without the protection of the embassy or the fiction of the trading organization, that did the most valuable work.

Placing "illegals" was a difficult matter. As they live and work under assumed identities, the first thing to do before an illegal can be put in place is to build an identity for the agent.

Operatives already in the foreign country would scour old obituaries and hospital records looking for infants who died 20, 30, even 40 years before. Then, they would check to see if there were any relatives of the long-deceased child still in the vicinity. If there weren't they would apply for a birth certificate in that name. Then, they would compile a fictitious history or "legend" for the spy, preferably a legend that couldn't be checked. The legend would say that the person had gone to a school that had, unfortunately, burned down several years before, and had worked at a business that had, unfortunately, gone out of business a few years back.

With the legend ready, a Soviet agent would be brought in to fill it. Once in place, the agents began the long slow work of infiltrating governments, scientific circles, industry, universities. They were the true Russian spies. And, many of these agents worked, not for the Cheka, but for a rival Soviet spy agency—the GRU.

THE GRU

People often make the mistake of equating the Central Intelligence Agency (CIA) with all American espionage, when in fact the CIA is only one of several agencies—such as the National Security Agency, the National Reconnaissance Office, the Defense Intelligence Agency—that spy for the United States. Similarly, it would be a mistake to equate the KGB or its predecessors with the entirety of the Soviet spy effort. The rival of the organs is the GRU—Glavnoye Razvedyvatelnoye Upravleniye—the Soviet agency for military intelligence. While the organs are concerned primarily with political intelligence, the objective of military intelligence is to find out what the other side is up to in its preparations for war.

After the revolution, as Trotsky put the Red Army together to fight the civil war, each unit within the army had its own intelligence unit. Trotsky's military intelligence operations came into almost immediate conflict with Dzerzhinsky's Cheka, especially over the agent networks—the Cheka wanted a monopoly over all spies. The Cheka did its best to intimidate the army intelligence operatives. The rivalry reached its heated peak when Chekists shot the entire military intelligence staff of the Eastern Front in July 1918.

The result was immediate disaster. The Red Army could not function without military intelligence. Trotsky went to Lenin and put his position very simply—either he was to have his own military intelligence organization or he would have to step down and Dzerzhinsky and the Cheka could take over the Red Army. Lenin didn't want to lose Trotsky. He told Dzerzhinsky to back off and allow Trotsky his military intelligence operation.

The struggle between the Cheka and military intelligence did not end there, however. At that point military intelligence was still fragmented—there was no single overall coordinating organization for the whole Red Army. Trotsky asked Lenin if he could form such an organization, but Lenin hesitated. He was afraid that Trotsky was getting too powerful as it was. Finally, however, he did give in to Trotsky's demands, partly because he was afraid Dzerzhinsky was getting too powerful. In the fall of 1918 the Cheka began the first wave of terror in response to the assassination attempt on Lenin in August. The terror was getting out of control, even for Lenin; he wanted to rein it in somewhat. One way to do that was to threaten Dzerzhinsky's monopoly over all intelligence matters by allowing Trotsky to set up a rival intelligence organization.

On October 21, 1918, Lenin signed a decree creating the Registrational Directorate of the Field Staff of the Republic. Known as the Registraupr, this was the first true version of what is now called the GRU—an overall Soviet military intelligence organization. But Lenin was still wary of Trotsky having too much autonomy, and so, he did something that continues to color the GRU to this day. He put in as head of the Registraupr a Chekist, Simon Ivanovich Aralov.

This was a brilliant stroke on Lenin's behalf. As a Chekist, Aralov was suspicious of the Red Army, but, working for military intelligence engendered in him a hatred for the Cheka. This kept the Registraupr off balance, unable to augment the power of either the Cheka or the Red Army. Indeed, torn between serving two masters, the Cheka or the Red Army, the Registraupr was more likely to align itself with a third master, the party, which is just what Lenin hoped. Lenin's ploy has become a virtual tradition. To this day the head of the GRU is almost always a high ranking veteran of the KGB.

The Registraupr began setting up foreign spying operations almost immediately. Whereas Dzerzhinsky and the Cheka were concerned with choking off anti-Bolshevik activity at home and abroad, the agents of the Registraupr focused on classical espionage—finding out what the other side is up to.

In those first few years after the revolution, there were countless potential agents to choose from. After the revolution there were an estimated 4 million foreigners in Russia, many of whom were dedicated communists, and there were thousands more streaming in every day from countries all around the world. It was a simple matter to send these people back to their homelands as spies. As well, the GRU used the agent provocateur technique Dzerzhinsky was using—sending spies, posing as czarists, White Russians or disaffected revolutionaries abroad to infiltrate the émigré groups. But, whereas Dzerzhinsky used these provocateurs to disrupt the émigré groups, the GRU used the émigré groups as covers for the agents to enable them to penetrate further into the host country.

The rivalry between the Cheka and the GRU continued throughout all of this. It reached another crisis in 1920 when the Soviet attempt to fire up a revolution in Poland failed. The failure was blamed on intelligence. Dzerzhinsky managed to deflect the blame off the Cheka and onto the shoulders of the GRU. To make his point he had several hundred GRU officers shot in November 1920.

Ironically, those executions marked the first time that many even in the party heard of the GRU. The GRU has always been more secretive than the organs. While every Soviet citizen knows what the KGB does, few are even aware that there is a GRU. Such is the nature of military intelligence—very few American citizens know about the National Reconnaissance Office—to be as secretive as possible.

The intense enmity between the GRU and the organs began when the GRU began. As we will see in later chapters, that enmity has yet to diminish.

THE END OF THE CHEKA

By early 1922 Dzerzhinsky had crafted the Cheka into a complete internal-external, domestic-foreign spying outfit.

It had the KRO for spying on Soviet citizens and foreigners in the Soviet Union, and it had the INO to run all the operations on the outside. The Cheka had, at that point, become the true model for what the KGB is today. It might seem surprising then that on March 1, 1922, the Cheka was abolished.

This, in fact, was as it had been planned. According to Bolshevik doctrine, Lenin had only created the Cheka to crush the immediate threat posed by the counter-revolutionaries. Once the civil war was over, there would be really no further need for the Cheka. At least that was the plan. What Lenin and Dzerzhinsky realized by 1922 was that the internal threat would never disappear; that there would always be counterrevolutionary forces within the Soviet Union that would have to be checked. Indeed, like so many Russian leaders before him, Lenin realized that the key to his and his successors staying in power was the organs.

And so, at the same moment that the Cheka ceased to exist, the State Political Administration—the GPU (Gosudarstvennoye Politicheskoye Upravleniye)—came into being. It was run under the jurisdiction of the People's Commissariat of Internal Affairs, the NKVD (Narodnyi Kommissariat Vnutrennikh Del). Dzerzhinsky was elected head of the NKVD. About 18 months later, on November 23, 1923, after the transformation of the revolutionary state into the Union of Soviet Socialist Republics, the GPU became the OGPU—the *Unified* (Obiedinyonnoye) State Political Administration and was taken out from under the NKVD. Naturally, Dzerzhinsky went with it.

The GPU-OGPU was even stronger than the Cheka, with even broader powers and fewer restraints. It also became even more cult-like. In the beginning, morale at the Cheka was not high. For one thing, many of the early Chekists were simply Ochrana agents that had either agreed to switch sides and work for Dzerzhinsky, or had been coerced into doing so—threats were often made against the families of ex-Ochrana agents.

Later, as the Cheka became the GPU, then OGPU, working for Dzerzhinsky's version of the organs became similar to what it must have been like to be a member of Ivan the Terrible's Oprichniki of centuries before. Recruits were sworn to the strictest secrecy and loyalty, and once on board, it was a job for life. Transgression and/or failure were punishable by death. To enforce the rules, agents were told to spy on each other.

Initiation into the GPU-OGPU was reportedly something like the old initiation into organized crime. If you were a recruit, in order to prove your dedication to the cause, you would be given an assignment to execute an "enemy of the people." If you failed, you would be killed.

But—as with the Oprichniki and the KGB of today—there were rewards for this work, and agents of the GPU-OGPU were accorded great status and privilege.

As much as the names changed—from Cheka to GPU to OGPU—the goals remained the same. One of Dzerzhinsky's primary tasks for the GPU-OGPU was to somehow trick the émigrés into returning home.

Dzerzhinsky knew that the only way he was going to lure anti-Bolshevik émigrés back to Russia would be by tantalizing them with the prospect of overthrowing Lenin and his cronies. To do this, Dzerzhinsky set up "The Trust."

The Trust was supposedly a trading agency, operating out of Moscow, that was trying to set up trade with other nations. Dzerzhinsky had word leak out that the Trust was really a front for anti-Bolsheviks who were plotting against Lenin. The Trust reached beyond the Soviet borders and made some tentative contact with the émigré communities.

Representatives of the Trust said they wanted to start a counterrevolution against the Bolsheviks, but that they would need the help of the émigrés. The émigrés were naturally suspicious. They were afraid that it was all a provocation of the GPU-OGPU's. So, the Trust had to prove itself. It did so by arranging for some key anti-Bolsheviks, hiding underground in the Soviet Union, to be smuggled out. It also smuggled some anti-Bolsheviks into Russia and then out again. By arranging for these safe passages, the Trust showed to the anti- Bolshevik émigrés that it could be trusted.

Dzerzhinsky was willing to allow these émigrés in and out of the country; he was after more important game. One of his prize catches was Boris Savinkoff. Savinkoff was a fellow revolutionary. Indeed, he had been one of the heads of the "Battle Organization" when Ievno Azeff was working his deceptions, but he had the unfortunate lack of foresight not to be in the Bolshevik camp after the revolution, and so had to flee the country. By the time Dzerzhinsky used the Trust to trick him back into the Soviet Union, Savinkoff had become a morphine addict. Dzerzhinsky convinced this broken man to betray everything he knew of the émigré plans for a counterrevolution.

One of the bigger game the Trust was after was Sidney Reilly. After working all sides of World War I—convincing the Russians to buy German arms while at the same time selling German secrets to the Russians—Reilly skipped out of Russia before the revolution. Reilly had a plan to return. He didn't respect the intelligence of the Chekists and so thought it would be possible to infiltrate the Cheka and set up a sort of shadow secret service within it. He believed that this shadow Cheka could take over when Lenin was ousted. Of course he saw himself at the head of this new agency.

Reilly was fooled by the Trust into thinking this was a possibility. He hooked up with its representatives in Paris. They suggested that he go to Russia to help with the counter-revolution. He followed the suggestion, and on September 25, 1925, using a fake passport, he left Finland and crossed into the Soviet Union.

Reilly intended it to be a short trip—just go in, make contact and get right back out again. He sent a postcard from Moscow on September 27. That was the last anyone outside of the Soviet Union ever heard of him.

Isvestia, a Soviet newspaper, reported a short time later that on the night of September 28-29, "four smugglers attempted to cross the Finnish border. Two were killed; one a Finnish soldier taken prisoner, and the fourth, mortally wounded, died on the way to Leningrad." One of the dead was later announced as having been Reilly.

The *Isvestia* story was a lie. Reilly hadn't been killed trying to flee to Finland—he didn't make it that far. In fact, he had been picked up by OGPU agents shortly after he met with members of the Trust. He was held prisoner in Moscow and interrogated.

Little is known about the ultimate fate of Reilly. Some reports indicate he was executed November 25, 1925; others say he was put to death the following June. Some maintain, however, that he was never executed, but that he remained alive— although insane—in prison, through World War II.

Some believe that the whole business was a ruse, a deception, and that Reilly had been a Soviet agent all along. He did reportedly betray many secrets to the Soviets that later allowed the Soviets to penetrate the British secret service and still later, the United States'. Whether Reilly gave up these secrets only under interrogation or because he wanted to or as an attempt to secure his freedom will never be known.

THE END OF AN ERA

By 1922, Lenin's health was failing. The question of a successor had not been resolved. Although Lenin had, to the world, painted a picture of himself as merely a figurehead of the communist party who acted at the behest of the people, in truth he had put himself in the position of an all-powerful dictator. The trouble with governments run by a single man is that when the man dies, the government can—and frequently does—collapse into chaos.

One of the reasons Lenin and Dzerzhinsky disbanded the Cheka and created the GPU was to make the Soviet organs more of an official institution. They hoped that the GPU-

OGPU would form the structure that would keep the Bolsheviks in power. It did the job. When Lenin finally died in 1924, the Soviet government did not collapse.

Felix Dzerzhinsky died on July 20, 1926. Some have ventured that he was lucky. Although he had supported Josef Stalin, Lenin's successor, in his ascension to the head of the party and the country, and had even helped Stalin consolidate his power, there is no telling how long he would have survived with Stalin in power. As Stalin's record with other chiefs of the OGPU will demonstrate, Dzerzhinsky might well have died with a bullet in the back of his head instead of dying in his bed.

3.

LIFE UNDER STALIN

Information on Stalin's early life is sketchy. He wanted it that way. Indeed, that's one of the reasons Dzerzhinsky was perhaps lucky that he died when he did. Stalin was intent on rewriting history to cast himself as hero of the revolution. So, over the years, people who knew Stalin from the early days of the movement, who knew the true role he played, often ended up dead.

Stalin was born Iosif Vissarionovich Dzhugashvili, on December 21, 1879, in the Georgian town of Gori. Georgia was a separate state within czarist Russia, as it is within the Soviet Union. The Georgians have a distinct language and culture, and they have always been slightly ostracized, treated like second- class citizens, by the Russian ruling elite. This angered Stalin, and his ruthless ambition can be explained in part by his desire to exact revenge on the Russians who ridiculed him as a Georgian peasant.

Indeed, he was a Georgian peasant. His childhood does not seem to have been a happy one. He was terrorized by a drunken father who beat him. Perhaps as a way of escape, young Josef (the anglicized form of Iosif) started on a religious path. He studied at the Tiflis Theological Seminary but left after a short while (according to his official biography, he was expelled for causing trouble, although his mother later said he left because of ill health).

Along with many young men of the day growing up under the oppressive regime of the czar, Josef became interested in the revolutionary movement, and in 1900 he joined the underground. Even then he was noted for his stridency

Josef Stalin, tyrannical ruler of the Soviet Union from 1924 to 1953. [Credit: UPI/Bettmann Newsphotos]

and his efforts to push his cohorts into ever more violent actions. When the revolutionary movement split into the Menshevik and Bolshevik groups, Stalin, given his tendency toward extremism, naturally fell in with Lenin and the Bolsheviks.

In the years leading up to 1910, Stalin was arrested and put in jail several times, but each time was fortunate to get off lightly. The fact that Stalin would prod his fellow revolutionaries into violent acts and then receive softer punishment than his cohorts gave rise to some speculation that he was, in fact, a provocateur for the czar's secret police, the Ochrana. If he did work for the Ochrana, the question is, who was he really serving? Was he a revolutionary spy, working his way into the Ochrana (as Sidney Reilly suspected) or was he an Ochrana agent trying to disrupt the revolutionary movement?

Like Lenin, who used an alias, Josef Dzhugashvili adopted a pseudonym. He chose Stalin, from *stal*, the Russian word for steel.

Although he never spoke perfect Russian, and had a thick Georgian accent, he was reasonably literate and worked for a short time on the communist party's newspaper, *Pravda*. He was then exiled to Siberia from 1913 to 1917. Upon his return from exile in 1917 he resumed work at *Pravda*, becoming its editor. When the revolution took place in the fall of 1917, Stalin played a relatively minor role, especially when compared to what Lenin or Trotsky contributed.

Stalin always resented Trotsky in particular for this, and this resentment would later cost Trotsky his life. While Stalin served in various positions in the communist party during the civil war, Trotsky was running the Red Army. But Stalin was an adept bureaucrat. He kept a fairly low profile and was rewarded for his diligence in party work by being elected as general secretary of the party in 1922, about the time that Lenin first became ill.

It was at this point that the future structure of the Soviet Union was being decided. With Lenin out of commission, Stalin began to press for a unified central government. Trotsky opposed him—he thought the system should be a federation, composed of individual republics. But Stalin managed to wrangle the support of a few key members of the Politburo who were jealous of Trotsky and it looked like he might win. But then Lenin regained some strength, joined with Trotsky against Stalin, and won. Revolutionary Russia became the Union of Soviet Socialist Republics.

But Stalin was by no means finished fighting. He may not have been a terribly intelligent man, but he was clever, intensely ambitious, and absolutely ruthless in his quest for power. He forged key alliances and maneuvered himself into position to take over the party leadership. Lenin and Trotsky tried to stop him, but Lenin died in 1924 and Trotsky could not defeat Stalin on his own. Trotsky's fight was finished when Dzerzhinsky closed ranks with Stalin— Dzerzhinsky saw which way the race for power was going and wanted to back the winning horse. At that point, with the OGPU behind him, Stalin was unbeatable.

When Dzerzhinsky died in 1926, Stalin had his first opportunity to pick the head of the OGPU. His choice was Vyacheslav Menzhinsky. Although he was a logical successor in some ways—he had been Dzerzhinsky's deputy—in other ways he was a strange choice for Stalin. Like Dzerzhinsky, Menzhinsky was a Pole, and Stalin generally didn't trust Poles. But what made Menzhinsky really such an odd choice to head Stalin's OGPU—and what made it odd that he was in any position of power—was that by any revolutionary standard he was a decadent man. He collected art, wore fine silks, seemed more interested in his piano playing than in running the OGPU, and, on occasion, gave himself manicures while conducting interrogations. Furthermore, he ridiculed the idea of the proletariat (the Marxist term for the working class) as "a stupidity discovered by the intelligentsia."

Menzhinsky's OGPU concentrated solely on internal operations and spying at home. He was reportedly uninterested in foreign espionage, considering it all—except for hard, scientific intelligence—to be a waste of time. In some ways this reflected Stalin's own feelings. He never trusted reports from his foreign agents, nor, in fact, did the

Genrik Yagoda, head of the NKVD, 1934-1936. Yagoda's brief reign as the organs' chief marked the beginning of the Stalinist terrors that claimed millions of lives. [Credit: UPI/Bettmann Newsphotos]

man he appointed to run foreign intelligence, Genrik Yagoda.

Yagoda couldn't have cared less about intelligence gathering. He was a tough Latvian peasant who considered it the mandate of the Special Division he ran to destroy all of Stalin's opponents. Yagoda put it simply (as quoted in *A History of the Russian Secret Service* by Richard Deacon): "The enemies of Stalin are the enemies of Russia. The Special Division is to ensure that no enemies of Stalin continue to live." Yagoda's agents were not spies so much as assassins then, who would track down the anti-Stalinists, wherever they may be, and kill them.

Menzhinsky lasted quite a long time—eight years—as the head of the OGPU, much longer than would have been expected of someone many regarded as weak and decadent, someone who Stalin reportedly abused and ridiculed for his failings. Why did Stalin keep him around so long? For one thing, Stalin was still not so powerful that he could sever all ties to the Dzerzhinsky era. He appointed as many of his own men—including the likes of Yagoda— to the OGPU as he could, and promoted them as fast as he could, but the organs were still filled with Dzerzhinsky men, such as Menzhinsky. When the time was right, Menzhinsky died— killed "mysteriously" in 1934. Trotskyites were initially blamed for the murder, but there was never any proof that they were involved. It is much more likely that Stalin was behind it.

1934 was an important year for the Soviet organs— Yagoda succeeded Menzhinsky, to become the first Stalinist at the head of the organs and the organs went under a name and organizational change. In 1923, when the GPU became the OGPU, it came out from under the jurisdiction of the NKVD—the People's Commissariat for Internal Affairs—to stand on its own. The NKVD then disappeared to a degree.

In 1934 the OGPU was given a new name, the Chief Directorate for State Security—GUGB—and it was brought back under a newly reconstituted NKVD. To the Soviet people, the parent organization overshadowed the subordinate and from then on the organs were know as the NKVD.

Being chosen by Stalin was no guarantee of job security— Yagoda lasted for only two years as the head of the NKVD. He disappointed Stalin more than once. The first time was over a counterfeiting scheme that Stalin had concocted. The Soviet Union was short of money, so Stalin proposed that they simply print up vast quantities of American currency. Yagoda was reluctant to enter into such a plot. Creating bills that would pass inspection was hard enough, but on the scale Stalin wanted, it would be almost impossible to elude detection for long. Yagoda did his best, having his agents steal the special paper that American currency was printed on, and the bills they did print up were virtually indistinguishable from real currency. But, as he had suspected, running such a large-scale operation, trying to distribute millions of these fake bills, proved impossible and the scheme came to a close. Stalin was not pleased.

It was Yagoda's second disappointment of Stalin that really caused his demise, however. It also triggered another onslaught of terror. Stalin was having trouble with Sergei Kirov, the communist party leader in Leningrad. Kirov was everything Stalin wasn't—namely smart and well-liked. Stalin feared him and wanted him dead. Yagoda—who had pledged that no enemy of Stalin should continue to live— was assigned the task of arranging Kirov's death. Kirov was killed on December 1, 1934, but the assassination was bungled to the extent that responsibility for the murder was laid at the doorstep of the NKVD. Stalin knew that the trail of responsibility would eventually wind its way to him. So, to cover for Yagoda and himself, he proclaimed that the murder of Comrade Kirov had been the dirty work of White Russian counterrevolutionary conspirators.

Josef Stalin shown voting in one of the Soviet Union's illusory elections. Voting next to him, the chief of the NKVD, Nikolai Yezhov, the "Bloody Dwarf," responsible for the deaths of millions. [Credit: UPI/Bettmann Newsphotos]

First, Stalin had everyone killed who knew anything about who really killed Kirov and why. Then, hundreds more—people with absolutely no connection to the Kirov plot—were also executed, and thousands of equally innocent citizens were imprisoned in camps, where death was just as certain, but slower. The circle of terror quickly expanded. Anyone who could even remotely be suspected of being a rival of Stalin's—that is to say, anyone who was smart, successful, or charismatic—was whisked away. Thousands more were executed or imprisoned. This kicked off a campaign of terror that rivaled the worst of what Lenin and Dzerzhinsky had perpetrated against the Soviet people.

Things were getting out of hand; even Stalin knew that. His only choice then was to blame his hatchet man—to point his finger at Yagoda. Yagoda was arrested in September 1936 and accused of every crime imaginable, including the recent excesses of the NKVD and the murder of Kirov. He was even charged with the murder of Menzhinsky.

As Yagoda's successor, Stalin brought in Nikolai Yezhov. Yezhov's job, supposedly, was to curb the excesses of the NKVD and to stop the wave of terror engulfing the land. Instead, he embarked on a program of terror that made Yagoda's pale in comparison. A short man, barely five feet tall, he became known as the "Bloody Dwarf." His method for curbing the excesses of the NKVD was to have it turn in upon itself. At least 500 high-level intelligence officers were executed. Gone was anyone who had a connection to the revolution. Here again was evidence of Stalin's paranoia that he would be ousted by people with better credentials than his own. Also on the hit list were Jews and any international communists in the ranks.

Then, when his purge of the NKVD was done, Yezhov turned his attention to the military, and there the stroke of his hand was much broader. Over 30,000 Red Army officers were executed in two years.

In 1938, as part of his purge of the NKVD, Yezhov ordered Yagoda, imprisoned in a cellar of the Lubyanka Prison, shot.

As it turned out, Yezhov himself didn't have much longer to live. He lost Stalin's trust. The man who had Stalin's trust—not a lot of it, but more than any other head of the organs—was Lavrenti Beria.

BERIA

Although several years younger than Stalin, Beria had many things in common with the tyrant. Born in 1898, he, too, was a peasant from Georgia—Beria was from Tiflis— who had inauspicious beginnings in the party. In fact, during World War I, Beria fought with the czar's army. But, he had, even then, ties with the movement, and began to establish his revolutionary credentials at an early age, or-ganizing the oil workers at Baku in 1918. By the age of 23 he was a spy for the Cheka, running intelligence gathering and anti-émigré operations in Prague and Paris, infiltrating the ranks of the White Russians and anti-Bolshevik plotters. He was good at this. He was an accomplished linguist and adept at socializing and mixing in with people in an unassuming manner.

He had been one of Stalin's appointees years before when Stalin was stocking the OGPU with men loyal to him. It was on the strength of this, and his own deft political maneuver-ing, that Beria managed to escape Yezhov's mass execution of key NKVD officers.

When Stalin told Beria to report to Moscow on July 28, 1938, he didn't know why he was being summoned. He feared—as anyone who Stalin summoned to Moscow feared—that he was in line for a bullet in the back of his head. To his surprise and undoubted relief he was instead ap-pointed as Yezhov's deputy and eventual successor. Yezhov was "promoted" to be the commissar of water transport— this would be like being "promoted" from being head of the CIA to the chief of the Bureau of Weights and Measures— and Beria became the head of the organs.

Beria's first action was to weed out everyone in the upper hierarchy of the NKVD who had been brought in by Yezhov or was in some way connected to him. This took a couple of months. Then, in December 1938, with his own men in place and the organs under his control, Beria accused Yezhov of being insane. Yezhov was summarily dismissed as commissar of water transport. He was arrested in the middle of the night and carted off to the Serby Psychiatric Institute. Accounts of his eventual demise vary. Either he was shot in the same Lubyanka cellar where Yagoda met his end or he was found dead one day at the Psychiatric Institute, apparently having committed suicide by hanging himself with his underwear.

Beria did not intend to suffer the same fate as his predecessors, and he didn't, at least not under Stalin. His simple tactic was to kowtow to Stalin, to be his staunchest, most outspoken supporter. First, he arranged great praise for Stalin. Stroking Stalin's insecurity about his position in the revolution, Beria had Soviet history rewritten, with Stalin placed at a level slightly higher than Lenin in the revolution's pantheon. Then, Beria gave Stalin credit for Beria's successes and when Stalin's policies failed, he had designated scapegoats take the blame.

But Beria had his own agenda beyond merely stroking Stalin's ego. He wanted power himself, and he got it. He broadly expanded the powers of the NKVD at home, and completely rebuilt the foreign operations. He, like everyone else in 1938, saw war on the horizon, and he wanted the Soviet Union's intelligence-gathering apparatus to be ready. The work of his predecessors in the field of foreign operations had been generally unimpressive.

There had been some success in seeding Britain with Soviet spies in the mid-1920s, but much of that success was lost in 1926 when Arcos, the Soviet trading organization and main spy front in London, was raided. The most important Soviet spy operation in Britain in the long term began in the late-1920s. That was when Soviet agents began to recruit spies at Cambridge University, one of the elite universities of England. Although this recruitment produced next to

Lavrenti Beria, in control of the organs from 1938 to 1953. In 1953, upon Stalin's death, he was in line to succeed the tyrant, but was outmaneuvered by Khrushchev and Malenkov and was shot. [Credit: UPI/Bettmann Newsphotos]

nothing in terms of immediate results, the long-term gains for the Soviets were impressive. One of the recruits was Harold "Kim" Philby, who rose very high within British intelligence circles over the succeeding decades, all the while working for the Soviets.

The most remarkable Soviet spy operation of the period began several years before Beria became head of the NKVD. It was a spy operation run by one man who in fact didn't work for the NKVD but for the GRU, Soviet military intelligence. Although this agent was arguably one of the greatest spies who ever lived, Stalin, quite characteristically, and to his peril, ignored many of this man's intelligence reports. His name was Richard Sorge.

RICHARD SORGE

In the 1950s and 60s, when Soviet leader Nikita Khrushchev tried to spruce up the image of the KGB he initiated public celebration of the spies of the past, painting them as heroes of the Soviet Union. The first Soviet spy to be so lionized was Richard Sorge, given the award of Hero of the Soviet Union. This honor was bestowed posthumously.

Sorge was born in Baku, in southern Russia, in 1895, but he grew up in Germany. He fought for Germany in World War I, was wounded quite seriously, and ended the war fighting on the Russian front. Although Sorge fought against Russians in the war, he was drawn to the revolutionary principles that were being discussed in Russia and was enthralled by the revolution in 1917.

After the war, Sorge studied at the Universities of Berlin, Kiel, and Hamburg, receiving a Ph.D. in political science at Hamburg in 1920. His interest in socialism had grown over the years (perhaps it was something in his blood—his grandfather had been a friend of Karl Marx) and by the early 1920s he was working for the German communist party.

He had a breadth of experience by that time—he'd been a coal miner, a teacher and a journalist—and had proven to be an accomplished linguist. He learned German as he grew up and his mother taught him Russian. He also picked up, over the years, English, French, Japanese, and Chinese. The Soviets got wind of him and in 1925 they contacted Sorge and invited him to Moscow. There he began training as a spy.

Sorge was in training for three years. In 1927 he went on a trial mission—he was sent to Hollywood to report on the film industry. He was sent in the guise of a German reporter. The mission went well; Sorge returned to the Soviet Union for some final training and in 1928 he became a full-fledged agent. He didn't work for the OGPU, however, but for military intelligence, the GRU.

He was sent to China to gather intelligence on Chiang Kai-shek's nationalist movement. Sorge decided, however, that what was going on in Japan was more important than what was happening in China; to Sorge it was the Japanese who posed the greatest threat to the Soviet Union in the east, not the Chinese. Although he set up his spy operation in Shanghai, he focused on Japan.

His cover was that of reporter for a periodical called *Soziologische Magazin*. As a journalist he was able to range far and wide over China, recruiting agents in all the major cities. His agents were Chinese, Japanese, Germans, and many Americans. He was especially popular among the Americans—he even adopted the cover of an American journalist, William Johnson, for a time. Among the Americans Sorge used was a woman, Agnes Smeadley. Sorge used Smeadley's apartment for his radio transmissions. Smeadley provided him with something even more important, however; she introduced Sorge to Ozaki Hozumi, the man who would become Sorge's chief contact in Japan.

Sorge felt that the Soviet Union had, to its peril, ignored Japan's military might. He felt that the British and the Americans had also largely ignored Japan (he thought that the Japanese could take the British colony in Singapore in three days). Trying to figure out how he could get even more intelligence on Japan, Sorge hit on a brilliant plan—he would infiltrate German operations in Japan and thereby gather information on both countries.

Sorge went to Berlin in May 1933. He joined the Nazi Party and began to work his way up in important circles. All this was done at incredible risk, for Sorge had grown up in Germany and had gone to university there; he was known and might be recognized. But he managed to pull it off and got what he desired—a posting to Japan as the Tokyo correspondent for a Frankfurt newspaper.

When Sorge arrived in Japan, Smeadley was waiting, already set up with her own cover. Sorge rose quickly within the German circles in Tokyo, ingratiating his way into the elite. He was allowed into the embassy and even became a close friend of the German ambassador. Some of the secret information he got a look at gave him advance warning of the German invasion of Poland in 1939, and, later, the German surprise invasion of the Soviet Union. Stalin initially ignored Sorge's reports as he did the reports of all secret agents, although, as Sorge's intelligence proved to be correct on more than one occasion, he did take some notice.

Sorge was a brilliant spymaster, maintaining an extensive network of spies. Furthering his reputation as a man who loved nothing more than a good time, Sorge would camouflage his meetings with his spies by throwing wild parties, complete with geisha girls. These parties drew attention from neighbors, but not from the Kempeitai, Japan's secret police. Early in the morning, when things had quieted down some, Sorge would talk with his agents, find out what they knew and give them new assignments.

Sorge's best agent was still Ozaki Hozumi. Hozumi had become friendly with several members of the Japanese cabinet and was the source of the single most important piece of intelligence to come from Japan as far as the Soviet Union was concerned. He found out that Japan was making plans for war against China but had no plans to attack the Soviet Union.

Sorge had tried to convince Stalin of this as early as 1936, even offering to put his life on the line in support of it. When the Japanese did attack China, Stalin was, for the first time, willing to believe that at least one spy might be trustworthy. Stalin still didn't trust Sorge when it came to intelligence regarding German intentions—Stalin had signed a nonaggression pact with the Germans and ignored advisors, including Sorge, who said Hitler would violate the pact and invade Russia anyway.

Germany invaded the Soviet Union (as Sorge had predicted) in June 1941. As the German troops marched northward that summer, a major question was whether or not Japan would attack in the East. According to Sorge's intelligence sources, most notably Ozaki, the Japanese were preparing to move into the Philippines and Southeast Asia; there were even rumors that they might attack British and American bases. This meant that Japan was ignoring the Soviet Union, and this allowed Stalin to redeploy troops in the East that had been waiting for the Japanese. Those troops were sent west and proved decisive in breaking the siege of Leningrad on December 7, 1941. That was the very same day, coincidentally, that the Japanese attacked the American naval base at Pearl Harbor in Hawaii. By the time that happened, however, Sorge was no longer sending back intelligence reports, and it was partly because of the attack on Pearl Harbor.

As Japan made its secret preparations for the surprise attack on the United States and war in the Pacific, the Japanese secret police, the Kempeitai, was working frantically to stop any leaks and to round up any foreign spies. The Kempeitai was suspicious of the German embassy. Although Germany was a friend and ally of Japan's, the embassy was something the Japanese couldn't control and they feared it could be used as a channel for secrets. So, they assigned agents to watch everyone who had dealings with the German embassy.

Richard Sorge (left), the Soviet master spy in the Far East in the years leading up to World War II, with his ace Japanese agent, Ozaki Hozumi (right). Sorge and Hozumi were arrested by the Japanese secret police in 1941 and were executed in November 1944. [Credit: UPI/Bettmann Newsphotos]

Sorge was dating a Japanese girl by the name of Kiyomi who had recently come into his life. He didn't know it, but she was a Kempeitai agent. Sorge knew he was under some suspicion, but he refused to keep a low profile and continued to probe and pry. The intelligence he was after was confirmation of the rumor that the Japanese were planning to attack American bases.

Not long after Sorge confirmed the surprise attack rumor, he took Kiyomi to a restaurant. It wasn't just for pleasure— the waiter at the restaurant was an intermediary who would pass information on to Sorge. Kiyomi watched as the waiter passed small balls of rice paper to Sorge. Unfolded, the pieces of paper contained messages. Sorge was supposed to read them, then burn them.

That night, the message told Sorge that the Kempeitai was on his trail. As they left the restaurant and drove off in a car, Sorge intended to burn the paper, but his lighter didn't work, so he just threw the paper out the window. Kiyomi asked Sorge to stop so that she could call her parents and let them know she would be late. Instead, she called the Kempeitai and told them where the secret message could be found. With that proof in their hands, they arrested Sorge the next day. By the end of October 1941 the entire Soviet spy network in Japan, including Ozaki Hozumi, had been rounded up.

The Germans at the embassy were flabbergasted. They didn't know that the Japanese had been spying on them and they refused to believe Sorge was a spy. In fact, they tried very hard to get Sorge released. But Sorge was never freed.

Sorge and Hozumi were kept in prison for several years. Eventually all their attempts to be freed were exhausted. Richard Sorge and Ozaki Hozumi were executed on November 7, 1944. Ozaki left behind some love poems for his wife. Sorge thanked his jailers for their kindness but said nothing else as he was escorted to the gallows.

The last piece of intelligence that Sorge had been able to smuggle out before he was captured in the fall of 1941 was that Japanese forces planned a surprise attack against the American naval base at Pearl Harbor on December 6—only one day off of the actual attack. If Sorge had been working for the Americans instead of the Soviets, World War II might have been a lot different.

THE GRU UNDER STALIN

Richard Sorge was working, not for the NKVD, but for the GRU— Soviet military intelligence. The period that he spied for the GRU—the 1930s—saw Soviet military intelligence reach its zenith and sink to its lowest point ever.

The GRU began to expand rapidly after Dzerzhinsky died. The mandate for the GRU was simple and far-reaching—it was to seek out any and all military plans and hardware around the world and steal them. By the early 1930s the GRU's budget for overseas operations was several times that of the OGPU's foreign budget.

The rivalry between the organs and military intelligence remained heated. It took a particularly nasty turn with the first wave of Stalinist purges carried out by Yagoda after the assassination of Kirov in December 1934. The purges reached far and wide, even into the foreign espionage field. With Yagoda on his way out, Stalin assigned GRU foreign operatives the ruthless task of killing off NKVD agents—the illegals—around the globe.

When Yezhov succeeded Yagoda, he accelerated the self-purging of the NKVD. Then, he turned on the Red Army, and after wiping out the entire general staff and thousands more, he brought his terror down on the GRU. Almost as a reprisal for the actions of the previous year, now it was the job of NKVD agents abroad to track down GRU illegals and kill them. At home, in Russia, the GRU was obliterated. Virtually everyone associated with the GRU was killed, right down to the cooks.

The GRU had to be rebuilt in its entirety. It struggled to its feet in 1937, and was back on track in early 1938. That just wouldn't do. On July 29, 1938, there was a second purge of the GRU and again it was completely eradicated. After Yezhov had destroyed it a second time, he took over as its chief. This may have been one of the reasons that Stalin had Yezhov removed—he was afraid of Yezhov once he had all the nation's secret police functions, both political and military, in his hands. Stalin could allow no one other than himself to have that much power, and so, Yezhov was killed.

The GRU remained in disarray. This had a dire effect in 1939-40 when the Soviets tried to take over Finland. The operation was a disaster, and the disaster could be blamed in part on a lack of military intelligence. At least Stalin saw it that way—he had the then head of the GRU, Lieutenant-General Ivan Proskurov, shot for incompetence. It is a mark of both Sorge's cleverness and his importance as a source of intelligence that throughout all of the purges and upheaval, he managed to survive and send back his invaluable reports.

MOKRIE DELA—"WET AFFAIRS"

While the GRU had spies such as Sorge gathering intelligence around the world, most of the NKVD's foreign effort was aimed at silencing the enemies of Stalin. Beria in particular aimed to create an atmosphere of fear, to have the threat of death hang over anyone who considered fleeing or betraying the Soviet Union. He let it be known that he had teams of assassins ready to track any traitor down. The message was: You can run, but you can't hide.

This kind of intimidation did not begin with Beria and it wasn't limited to Soviet citizens. The Soviets were murdering anyone who stood in the way of their goals from fairly early on. Over the years, some of the most frequent targets have been leaders of other nations, especially those nations that the Soviet Union wants to dominate. In 1926, the OGPU, under Stalin, shot a Ukrainian leader in Paris and kidnapped and killed an Estonian leader visiting Moscow. Also murdered, of course, were any White Russians, czarists, disgruntled émigrés, and disloyal communists, as well as intelligence agents who failed or didn't do what they were told.

This kind of work—liquidating people—was known as *mokrie dela*, or "wet affairs," so called that because they involved the spilling of blood. For many years *mokrie dela* were carried out on an ad-hoc basis; whenever they needed doing, they were done by whoever was available. In 1936, however, the NKVD formed the Administration of Special Tasks, specifically to carry out this kind of nasty business. The Administration of Special Tasks quickly became known by the more accurate moniker of "Execution Squad."

The Execution Squad was run directly from Moscow, perhaps on Stalin's personal approval. He didn't want to assign assassinations to local agents, afraid that they would bungle the job. The work would be given to the Squad, which would be quickly dispatched.

Two of the first victims of the Squad were a rogue Soviet agent hiding out in Lausanne, Switzerland, and an ex-Soviet diplomat living in Paris. The Execution Squad was particularly busy in Spain during the Spanish Civil War of the 1930s. The Squad employed Otto Katz, a failed Czechoslovakian theatrical producer, as their "finger man"—he would point out the "enemies" and the Execution Squad would do its work.

Two special targets of the Execution Squad were Alexander Orloff and Walter Krivitsky. Orloff, once the head of the Cheka's Economic Section, was sent by the NKVD to Spain to gather economic intelligence. While he was there he saw the workings of the Execution Squad and was appalled—so appalled that he rebelled against the NKVD and Stalin and began to publish articles denouncing them. He was lucky; he escaped the wrath of Stalin and his executioners and later published a book titled *The Secret History of Stalin's Crimes.*

Leon Trotsky, builder of the Red Army, shown here in exile in Mexico in 1938, two years before he was assassinated by an agent of the organs. [Credit: UPI/Bettmann Newsphotos]

Walter Krivitsky was not so lucky. He had been an important figure in the Soviet Union's pre-war intelligence-gathering efforts. He had been Resident Director for the NKVD in Vienna and later, Holland. Eventually, like Orloff, he too rebelled. He hated Stalin and all that the tyrant had done to pervert the goals of the revolution. Krivitsky defected, first to France, and then to the United States, ending up in Washington. He was found dead, an apparent suicide, on February 11, 1941. Some think that he was murdered, that his killer forced him to write his suicide notes at gunpoint then killed him.

The Execution Squad's most important target was Leon Trotsky.

THE ASSASSINATION OF LEON TROTSKY

Why was Stalin so obsessed with Trotsky? Because Trotsky was the man who, by all rights, should have led the Soviet Union after Lenin died.

One thing Stalin and Trotsky had in common is that neither were ethnic Russians. Trotsky was born in the town of Yanovka in the Ukraine, on November 7, 1879, making him the same age as Stalin. His real name was Lev Davidovich Bronstein. In 1896 he was drawn into the underground revolutionary movement and began to read Marx. He was arrested in 1898 and sentenced to four-and-a-half years of prison and exile in Siberia. He escaped from Siberia using a passport bearing the name Leon Trotsky. He adopted the name from then on.

In the 1903 Menshevik/Bolshevik split, Trotsky sided with the more liberal Mensheviks, who believed in democratic socialism. Despite their ideological differences, however, Trotsky and Lenin were acquaintances during this period and worked together on a revolutionary newspaper.

When the czarist government was brought down in March 1917 and eventually replaced by the provisional government organized by Kerensky, Trotsky still counted himself a Menshevik. He, like other Mensheviks, supported the provisional government as the first step toward a new, democratic, socialist Russia. In the summer of 1917, however, Trotsky was in a sense betrayed by the Kerensky government, which he had supported when he was arrested during a crackdown on Bolsheviks. Enraged, he joined the Bolsheviks while still in prison.

During the revolution in November he led the military. He kept this role throughout the civil war, fashioning the Red Army out of the rag-tag remnants of the czar's army.

Trotsky was everything Stalin wasn't; he was a brilliant revolutionary thinker and a thoughtful and respected man. He was one of the first five members of the Politburo, which was created in 1919. As the head of the Red Army, he wielded immense power but he never used it to try to seize personal control of the country. Trotsky never lost his Menshevik leanings. He always fought for greater liberalization, for more democracy, and more of a free-market economy.

Lenin, by taking personal control of the state, had set in place the potential for one-man totalitarian rule. After he recovered from his first stroke, he fought along with Trotsky to liberalize the government and keep Stalin out of power. But Stalin had been gathering allies over the years, including Dzerzhinsky, and when Lenin died, Trotsky was all alone. He fought against Stalin by himself, but he lacked the support to succeed. He was removed from his position as head of the military in January 1925. In a wave of anti-Semitism (Stalin hated Jews almost as much as Hitler did) in 1926, Trotsky was expelled from the party, and in 1928 was exiled to Central Asia. He was finally expelled from the Soviet Union altogether in 1929.

Trotsky lived in various countries before settling in Mexico in 1936. He was traced there by Stalinist agents, who found him living in a villa in Coyocan, near Mexico City. No move was made to kill him immediately, but there was a trail of death leading to him. The Execution Squad had most likely been involved in the death of Trotsky's son, Leo Sedoff, and his associate, Rudolf Klement, whose

Ramón Mercader, a.k.a. Jacques Mornard, assassin of Trotsky, shown in prison as he receives his 20-year sentence. [Credit: UPI/Bettmann Newsphotos]

decapitated corpse was found in the Seine in France in 1938. The next and final step was to kill Trotsky himself.

Beria wanted the assassination done in such a way that it couldn't be traced to the NKVD. The first two attempts were disasters, hopelessly bungled. In the first attempt, the attackers, after being unable to kill Trotsky, ended up kidnapping Trotsky's American secretary, Robert Sheldon Harte. Harte was later murdered (perhaps to keep him quiet if, as some suspect, Harte was involved in the plan). The second attempt, in May 1940, featured bombs and machine guns, but the assassins were driven off by Trotsky's bodyguards.

Beria was not pleased. He decided that tactics should be switched and that they should go for a more subtle approach, having an agent insinuate his way into Trotsky's inner circle and then kill him. Beria asked his head of the Execution Squad in Spain to recommend such an agent. A women, Maria Caridad del Rio Mercader, volunteered. She was a fanatical communist and would do whatever Moscow wanted done. Beria, however, refused to send a woman on such a mission. So, Maria suggested that they use her son Ramón. Beria accepted the idea.

Ramón, under the name of Jacques Mornard, worked his way into the Trotskyite circles in Paris. After building up his credentials as a devoted follower of Trotsky, he traveled to Mexico in disguise, using a fake Canadian passport. Once in Mexico he befriended a friend of Trotsky's and gained access to the aging revolutionary himself. But he did not kill Trotsky right away, and this annoyed Beria greatly.

Ramón had been supplied with an American car and a great deal of cash and Beria was afraid that Ramón was taking it easy, enjoying himself. So he threatened Ramón's family, telling him to kill Trotsky as soon as possible and escape. If he wasn't able to escape, he was to kill himself.

Ramón went to visit Trotsky on August 20, 1940. He pulled out a mountain climber's ice axe and clubbed Trotsky in the head. The wound was fatal. Trotsky's bodyguards heard the yelling and came running. Ramón was captured, but instead of killing himself as Beria had ordered, he said: "I had to kill because they forced me to do it . . . they are holding my mother prisoner."

Trotsky died the next day. Stalin was finally free of the threat, the specter, of his most feared enemy.

Ramón Jacobo del Rio Mercader was found guilty of murder and sent to prison with a 20-year sentence. Although he had done the job Beria wanted done, his blurted confession and implication of the NKVD was a potentially fatal error. Mercader spent his days in prison terrified that Beria would exact revenge, but no attempt was made on his life. When he was eventually released from prison in 1960, he disappeared, reportedly turning up in Czechoslovakia.

LITTLE CHICAGO

Imagine a typical mid-western American town, just before World War II, a town with everything such a town should have, right down to the roller rink, the kind you'd find within an hour's drive of any major city. Now imagine that the major city is Moscow, and that all the townspeople are actually Soviet spies in training. Welcome to Little Chicago, part of the Soviet Academy for Spies at Bykovo, situated 40 miles outside the Russian capital.

While the main thrust of the foreign operations conducted under Beria was to track down and kill the enemies of Stalin, his NKVD also turned out scores of traditional spies. Beria had two goals for these agents: he wanted to put agents in place who, like Sorge, could help win the coming war; he also wanted to put agents in place that could, over the years, work their way into important positions in their new host countries.

It was these latter agents, the ones that were to establish "deep cover," that were trained at Little Chicago. The main destinations for these agents were the United States and Canada. Beria demanded total linguistic authenticity, and total knowledge of American and Canadian customs and ways of doing things. He wanted his agents to be able to pass for Americans without question. They had to have the right facial expressions and body language; they had to know all about baseball and what to put on a hot dog at the ballpark; they had to develop an appetite for apple pie. Little Chicago was as up-to-date as possible. The roller rink was added to Little Chicago after a Soviet spy in the US who didn't know how to roller skate was taken to a roller rink by his new American friends and was injured.

With war approaching, Beria needed as many agents as he could get. He began a massive recruitment drive, seeking out the top Soviet university students, members of the police force, even the top Russian actors and actresses of the day. Once they had been trained at Bykovo, they were sent to the United States and Canada under an identity created for them. There, they would enter US and Canadian universities to study science and technology so that they could later get jobs either in the government or with military contractors.

These agents—sometimes called "sleepers"—might not be contacted by their Soviet spy bosses for years, until they had reached a position where they could get access to secrets. These deep-cover agents were the ultimate "illegals." And Bykovo hasn't stopped producing them. Some estimate that to this day, as many as 100 to 200 Bykovo graduates enter the United States and Canada each year.

While Beria was planning for the future by putting the sleepers in place, he also had the more immediate and pressing concern of the coming war.

4.

THE WAR YEARS AND THE END OF STALIN

The world was stunned when Stalin signed the nonaggression pact with Germany in August 1939. Communists in a pact with fascists? According to social and political ideology, the Soviets and the Nazis were fundamentally and diametrically opposed. Communism holds that everyone is equal in the state, and that everyone should share power and profit equally. Fascism holds that there should be an elite, ruling class that dictates the lives of the people.

In practice, of course, the Soviet Union under Stalin and Germany under Hitler were quite similar. In each country one party (the communist party in the USSR; the National Socialist, or Nazi party in Germany) ran everything; all freedoms were suspended; and citizens were imprisoned and later put to death in horrifying numbers because of the fears of the ruling elite (in Germany, Jews and other minorities were exterminated so they wouldn't "pollute the race;" in the Soviet Union anyone deemed even remotely to be an enemy of Stalin's was dealt with similarly). Still, the world was astonished when Stalin and Hitler entered into an agreement not to attack each other.

Stalin tried to explain the pact by saying that the other countries of Europe were no better than Germany and that any grievances the Germans had with those other countries was none of the USSR's business. Whether or not he actually believed that, the real reason Stalin signed the pact was because he feared that if war broke out the Soviet Union would be defeated. He was even willing to ignore all the evidence that showed that Hitler wouldn't live up to the pact and would invade Russia when he was ready to do so.

German troops crossed into Poland in September 1939 and World War II began. The Soviet Union managed to stay out of the conflagration until June 1941, when Hitler lived up to everyone's—except Stalin's—expectations and sent his armies into Russia. Because of Stalin's obstinate refusal to believe that this would happen, the USSR was woefully unprepared for the war and the Germans made rapid advances.

Beria, however, was not caught completely off guard. There were agents other than Richard Sorge who told him what was about to happen.

The most successful Soviet spy operation in Europe in the years leading up to the war was the "Lucy Ring" in Switzerland. "Lucy," the head of the ring, was actually Rudolph Roessler, a German publisher who was opposed to the Nazi regime and left Germany for Switzerland when the Nazis came to power in the 1930s.

Although Switzerland remained neutral throughout the war it had its own intelligence service, and when war broke out, Roessler was signed on as one of the chief analysts for Swiss intelligence. Roessler, however, did not want to remain neutral; he wanted to do everything he could to help those who were fighting against the Nazis. And so he sold secret intelligence to the Soviets.

The information he sold them was incredibly valuable. Roessler had a virtual pipeline connection to the German High Command and was able to tell Moscow what the Germans' next moves on the Eastern Front would be—not that Stalin was always ready to believe the reports.

How did Roessler get such information? He told the Soviets things that Swiss intelligence simply wasn't capable of bringing in. It is believed that Roessler had a secret source in the German High Command. According to one theory, 10 dissident anti-Nazi Bavarian generals who Roessler had served with in World War I were his source. Others believe that Roessler's leak was none other than Martin Borman, Hitler's deputy.

Roessler also received intelligence from another source. Interestingly enough, it was a source he wasn't aware of— the British. The British wanted to help the Soviets, but couldn't do so directly because of the atmosphere of distrust and suspicion that Stalin had created. The British knew the Soviets wouldn't accept British help, suspecting some hidden motive, some plot. So, the British would pass on whatever intelligence they had gathered about Germany that concerned the Soviets through Swiss intelligence (the Swiss were willing to take free intelligence about the Germans, despite their official neutrality), knowing that Roessler would pass it on to the Russians.

The Lucy Ring was finally broken in May 1943 by a pair of German double agents, George and Joanna Wilmer, who had penetrated Swiss intelligence. By that time the damage had been done, however, and the tide of the war was rising against the Germans. It's a sign of the unspoken support the Swiss had for Roessler and other anti-Nazi spies that these spies were all given short sentences and were treated well.

But not all of the agents of the organs in the war years were involved in the war effort. Many of Beria's agents were still fighting the hideous war Stalin had been waging for years against his own people.

THE WAR AT HOME

When Germany invaded the Soviet Union on June 22, 1941, one of Stalin's greatest worries was that the Germans, as they marched across the countryside, would free labor-camp prisoners and that these prisoners would join the Germans in fighting the Red Army. So one of Stalin's priorities was to move the camps as far from the battle front as possible. If there wasn't time to move a camp before the Germans reached it, the prisoners were simply shot.

As the war threw the country into turmoil, dissident anti-Soviet groups of Russians sprang up and it was Beria's job to crush them. Beria fought back with an onslaught of agent provocateurs who would infiltrate the groups and destroy them from within.

He reportedly sent his men, dressed up as soldiers of the SS (the branch of the German military that used the most brutal terror techniques and was the instrument Hitler used in his effort to annihilate the Jews), into Russian villages near the front to rape, murder, and set buildings on fire. The goal was to make sure that the invading Germans would not be seen as saviors.

When that didn't work, when the anti-Soviet partisan groups couldn't be stopped either by encouragement, propaganda, or the work of provocateurs, Beria had one final technique to use to crush them: he would surreptitiously leak to German intelligence the whereabouts of these anti-Soviets, identifying them in a way that would make the Germans think they were either anti-German guerrillas or worse, saboteurs posing as anti-Soviet partisans. In either case, the Germans would then wipe them out, doing Beria's work for him.

And, of course, after the war, anyone who was discovered to have been part of an anti-Bolshevik partisan group was shot.

In the James Bond books and movies, Agent 007 is always coming up against "Smersh," a particularly vicious Soviet organ that is responsible for murdering the spies of other countries. There really was a Smersh, and its name, a contraction of *smert shpionam*, means "Death to spies." But, when Beria created Smersh in April 1942, the "spies" he was concerned with were not the likes of James Bond but everyday Soviet citizens who might be suspected of working for the Germans.

Almost anything could make one a suspected spy. Just living in a town that had been overrun by the Germans was enough. After the Germans retreated and the village returned to Russian control, everyone in the village was a potential suspect. Thousands were shot by agents of Smersh, and hundreds of thousands more were sent to the camps. Smersh also operated like the OO of the Cheka, working in the rear of the Red Army as it advanced, shooting all those who fell behind.

Distrust ran so high that many Soviet prisoners of war who managed to escape from the Germans or who were released as the Germans retreated, were shot as suspected spies. Smersh was disbanded in March 1946, possibly because by that time most of the people who could be suspected of treason were dead.

Beria also used the cover of the chaos of the war to mount two devastating operations against Poland that helped bring it under the Soviet sphere of influence at the end of the war.

The Soviets wanted the Polish communists to be in power at the war's conclusion, but for that to happen, the Polish independent leadership would have to be destroyed. And so, agents of the USSR executed an estimated 15,000 Polish officers and buried the corpses in mass graves in the Katyn forest. The Soviets then assigned blame for the massacre to the German SS.

When Germany invaded Poland in September 1939, thousands upon thousands of Poles fled their country to form an army in exile. During the war, Polish soldiers and pilots became known as some of the fiercest and most courageous fighters in the Allied forces. The leader of the Polish forces was General Wladislav Sikorsky. He was the one man who could possibly have forged an independent Poland, one free of Soviet domination, at the end of the war. Therefore, he was a primary target of Beria and the organs.

In the first few days of July 1943, Sikorsky left Allied command in London to visit the Polish troops stationed in North Africa. On the way back, on the night of July 4, the plane carrying Sikorsky stopped in Gibraltar to refuel. Not long after the plane took off again, as it climbed to its flying altitude, an altimeter switch, a fuse that is triggered by a rise in altitude, set off a bomb that blew Sikorsky's plane out of the sky. Beria's agents had done their job.

THE GRU DURING THE WAR

Stalin's nonaggression pact with Hitler in August 1939 set the stage for one of the most bizarre stories in the history of Soviet military intelligence.

In the 1930s, the GRU recruited a large number of spies in Germany. Most of these spies were card-carrying communists—members of their national communist party. One of the basic rules of being a GRU agent is that one can no longer be an acknowledged communist. These recruited spies were asked to burn their communist party cards. They balked. They would do it, they said, only if they were granted membership in the communist party of the Soviet Union. Their GRU controllers agreed, but said that for security, their CPSU cards would remain in Moscow.

These agents worked hard and well for the GRU, keeping it apprised of many important German military developments. It wasn't long, however, before the Nazis got wind of the spies and were on their trail. A group of the spies fled Germany and finally ended up in Moscow. They were then arrested on suspicion of being German agents. They protested that they were members of the CPSU, but there was no record of them; no cards had ever been issued. These agents were being imprisoned by the country they had been risking their lives for. Their situation worsened.

In 1939, when Hitler and Stalin signed their nonaggression pact, part of the deal was that Stalin would get his hands on a few of Germany's most advanced military fighter planes, and Hitler's secret police, the dreaded Gestapo, would, in return, get its hands on the GRU spies. But Stalin felt the GRU spies then in jail knew too much and might tell the Germans details of GRU operations. So, the Soviets and the Germans worked out a unique deal. The Gestapo was given permission to meet the spies in Moscow, to speak to them just long enough to determine they were the ones they were looking for.

On the appointed day, the GRU trotted out these loyal agents and lined them up outside the Kasheirski Electric Power Plant in Moscow. The Gestapo compared them to the photographs they had of the spies, confirmed that they were indeed the men the GRU said they were, and, with representatives of the CPSU and GRU looking on, shot them. Together the CPSU, GRU, and Gestapo representatives burned the bodies in the furnaces of the power plant.

The romance between Stalin and Hitler came to an end when German troops invaded the Soviet Union in June 1941. The GRU was still trying to put itself together after the ravages of the purges. The new chief was General Filipp Golikov. Golikov was one of the few chiefs of the GRU who died a natural death—six of his seven predecessors and several of his successors have had their career ended by a bullet. His longevity is a testament to his success both as chief of the GRU and as a military leader. He only ran the GRU during the early part of the war, but during that time he oversaw his agents' penetration of the German general staff.

During the war the GRU was split in two. One half handled strategic intelligence—getting agents into the US and Britain, working toward long-term intelligence goals—and the other half handled operational intelligence—the day-to-day, tactical intelligence needed by the army to fight the war. These two halves were merged after the war.

It was after the war that the animosity between the GRU and the organs revived. It was then that the GRU once again became a player in the relentless power struggle among the Soviet hierarchy.

THE ATOM BOMB SPIES

Beria's agents during the war had done well in America. He had agents penetrate the OSS (America's wartime spy agency) up to the mid-level, and he had men in the Depart-

Klaus Fuchs, British scientist who passed vital atom bomb secrets to the Soviets in the 1940s. [Credit: UPI/Bettmann Newsphotos]

ments of War (now Defense), State, Navy, Commerce, Interior, and Treasury. But Stalin wanted more, and he was most concerned with reports of a "super weapon"—the atomic bomb.

The Soviets already had a couple of British scientists on their payroll, as well as Donald Maclean—one of the Cambridge University students recruited in the 1930s—who had access to some atomic secrets. The biggest results, however, came from two scientists—Allan Nunn May and Klaus Fuchs.

Nunn May, a Canadian, was at the heart of where key work was being done—Canada would be supplying much of the uranium for atomic research in the United States. Canada was the focus of the Soviets for other reasons. For one, Canada was slightly easier to penetrate than the US and made a perfect entry point for Soviet agents being sent to America. From 1943, when Colonel Nicholai Zabotin was sent in to head the Soviet spy operation in Ottawa, Soviet espionage activities in the US and Canada were coordinated from Canada's capital.

There was a network of highly placed traitors and Soviet agents throughout Canada and the United States. Among them were Julius and Ethel Rosenberg.

Although the Rosenbergs were undoubtedly spying for the USSR—passing on atomic secrets gathered for them by Julius' brother-in-law, David Greenglass, who worked at the Los Alamos facility in New Mexico where the world's first atomic bombs were made—it is questionable whether or not the secrets were all that important. The secrets did contain information on the "lens" of the atomic bomb—the mechanism used for detonation—but most of the intelligence usually concerned things that the Soviets probably already knew. The Soviets had their own atomic weapons

Julius and Ethel Rosenberg, shown after their conviction for passing atom bomb secrets to the Soviets. While there has been some controversy over the years as to whether or not the Rosenbergs were really guilty, the preponderance of evidence does indicate that they were spying for the Soviets, although the information they passed on may not have been of great value. They were executed for their crime. [Credit: UPI/Bettmann Newsphotos]

program, beginning before the war, and although it was nowhere near as far along as the American program, it was still considerably advanced. The Soviets did, however, learn a great deal from Nunn May and Fuchs—from Fuchs in particular.

Fuchs had in fact sought out the Soviets when he was in Britain. He knew the potential of the atomic research program, and when he found out that the Soviets, because they didn't have much to offer and couldn't be trusted, were not to take part in the joint venture with the US, Britain and Canada, he decided to do something about it. The most valuable intelligence he gave to the Soviets concerned the failures the Americans had encountered—he didn't tell the Soviets what to do but what not to do. He told them what experiments to avoid, what avenues to ignore. This saved the Soviets a great deal of time and money.

In the end, of course, the Soviets would have eventually built their own bomb without having to resort to espionage, but this way they did it faster. According to various estimates, the atom bomb spies saved the Soviet nuclear research program from 18 months to four years.

The atom bomb spy ring came crashing down on the Soviets in 1945 when, as a complete surprise, Igor Gouzenko, a Soviet cipher clerk at the embassy in Ottawa, defected. He went to the security service wing of the Royal Canadian Mounted Police (RCMP) and told all he knew about the spy ring in the US and Canada. This led, in short order, to several arrests. The Rosenbergs were eventually executed for treason in the United States. Fuchs was not arrested until 1949, by which time he had returned to Britain.

THE FALL AND RISE OF LAVRENTI BERIA

During the war, the organs underwent several name and organizational changes. In 1941, when, because of its operation of the ever-growing forced-labor programs, the NKVD had become too huge, it was relieved of its intelligence-gathering and secret police functions, which were taken over by a new agency, the People's Commissariat for State Security—NKGB (Narodnyi Kommissariat Gosudarstvennoy Bezopastnosti).

In 1946, as the country tried to recover from the war, both the NKVD and the NKGB were elevated to the status of ministries, becoming the MVD—Ministry for Internal Affairs (Ministerstvo Vnutrennikh Del)—and the MGB—Ministry for State Security (Ministerstvo Gosudarstvennoy Bezopastnosti). Beria was promoted, and finally given a spot in the Politburo. He was replaced at the MVD by Lieutenant General Sergei Kruglov. But Kruglov was more Stalin's man, and Beria's "promotion" to the Politburo turned out to be a way for Stalin to get him out of the way and reduce his power.

It was not long after this that Beria suffered a truly major setback when Stalin and his foreign minister, Vyacheslav Molotov, decided to create one agency to run foreign espionage operations and formed the KI, or Committee for Information (Komitet Informatsii), in 1946.

Stalin was wary of Beria, and he had every reason to be. Beria was making a play for power. He wanted to be in position to take over as leader of the country when Stalin died. Since Stalin's health had been failing for several years, that was a strong possibility. But the Soviet dictator's moves against him had put Beria's plans in jeopardy. Beria had to get himself back on top.

His first task was to weaken the power of the KI. To do that, he had to wrest some control of foreign operations away from them. In 1948, despite the intense rivalry between the organs and the GRU, Beria arranged for the GRU to regain control over its own foreign operations.

The next step was to go after the individual men who stood in his way. Kruglov, at the head of the MVD—Ministry of the Interior—was Stalin's man and somewhat unassailable.

Abakumov at the MGB was a different story. Beria's weapon against him was Stalin's own notorious paranoia.

In 1951, Beria, with the help of powerful fellow Politburo member Georgi Malenkov, and the GRU, convinced Stalin that Abakumov had covered up evidence of a plot against the great leader. Plots were Stalin's obsession; he was convinced that people were constantly conspiring against him (as indeed they probably were). With a hint of suspicion attached to his name, Abakumov was doomed. Stalin had Abakumov booted from the MGB and arrested.

Beria reasserted his position as Stalin's trusted security chief. Stalin even went along with Beria's wishes and broke up the KI in the fall of 1951. The foreign operations that the KI had controlled were returned to the MGB. Beria had returned to his stature of the war years.

As further evidence of the never-ending enmity between the GRU and the organs, once Beria was back as head of the organs, he had the leadership of the GRU purged, even though the GRU was partly responsible for removing Abakumov and getting Beria back into power.

Beria was now again in position to succeed Stalin. All Stalin had to do was die.

Stalin, of course, did die, and, for the Soviet people, not a moment too soon. In January 1953 his rampant paranoia reached new heights when he "uncovered" the "Doctor's Plot." He became convinced that a group of Moscow doctors, mostly of Jewish descent (Stalin was a notorious anti-Semite) were conspiring to kill him. Stalin responded with his usual ruthlessness. He had scores of doctors rounded up and shot. It looked like the Soviet Union was about to undergo another wave of Stalinist terror. But, fortunately for the world, Stalin's health was fast declining. On March 2, 1953, he died. It is now believed that Beria saw Stalin suffer a stroke but forbade the guards from summoning medical help, telling them that the leader was just resting.

While there was a certain amount of relief in the Kremlin when Stalin died, there was also an overriding sense of panic. Beria was poised to seize power, but it was not quite within his grasp. The Soviet Union stands on three legs—the party, the Red Army and the organs. Beria's first goal was to consolidate his power over the organs. Kruglov, who had been unassailable when Stalin lived, was ousted by Beria from the top of the MVD. Ignatiev at the MGB was soon to follow. Beria then brought the MVD and MGB back together as they had been in the days when he ran the NKVD.

With this consolidation of power Beria now had a third of the country under his personal supervision. He controlled the internal security police, all foreign espionage operations except those run by the GRU, the 300,000 Border Guards, the labor camps, the regular police (called the militia), and the nuclear weapons and missile programs. Beria was in a favorable position. He told all his foreign operatives to lay low and not get into any trouble. He didn't want any international incident to provide his foes within the party with the ammunition they needed to bring him down. He set to work on widening his power base.

Beria couldn't make any inroads into the military but wasn't worried. He felt that the Red Army, while not supporting him, would also not work against him. The question was whether or not he could gain control of the party.

There were three powerful men in the Politburo that Beria had to contend with. One was Georgi Malenkov, the new premier, who earlier had allied himself with Beria to get Abakumov out of the MGB; he was no longer an ally. Another was Molotov, one-time foreign minister and first head of the short- lived KI. He also was no ally. Lastly, there was Nikita Khrushchev, a fast-rising figure in the party.

Beria couldn't fight Malenkov and the others directly so he tried to isolate them and all the aging party bosses. He did this by declaring a security emergency. Because of the emergency, there would be no meetings of the Central Committee or of the Politburo. Beria then tried to use the technique of "divide and conquer," by wooing the Central Committee members, one by one, over to his side.

At this point, Malenkov, Molotov, and Khrushchev must have been frightened, not merely for their political future, but for their lives. Word came through their informers that Beria intended to seize control on June 19.

On June 17, they were blessed with what for them turned out to be a very fortuitous event. There was an uprising in East Berlin. People were rioting in the streets against the communist dictatorship that controlled their country.

Rivals to succeed Stalin, Lavrenti Beria and Georgi Malenkov, are pallbearers of Stalin's casket. Beria is on the left side of the casket, at the front. Malenkov is right behind him. Beria would be dead within the year. [Credit: UPI/Bettmann Newsphotos]

Maybe this is something that Beria could never have foreseen. Maybe he would have, had he been paying more attention to doing his job rather than fighting for power. At any rate, as head of all internal and external security for the Soviet Union, it was something that his enemies could point to and say he should have foreseen.

Malenkov was able to override Beria's emergency declaration with one of his own. An emergency meeting of the Central Committee was called and Beria was ordered to appear before it to account for the uprising in East Berlin. At least that was the pretext for the meeting. Beria did as he was ordered, but what actually happened after he walked through the doors into the meeting on June 26 is a mystery.

On Christmas Eve, 1953, *Pravda* announced that Lavrenti Pavlovich Beria, former head of the NKVD, had been shot. He was charged with, among other things, being a foreign spy. There is, however, some question about Beria's fate. That he was shot there is little doubt. *When* he was shot is a different matter. The official story has it that Beria was arrested after the meeting and held in prison until he was put on trial from December 18 to 23, and then executed on the 23rd along with several of his deputies.

According to another story, however, not long after Beria went through those meeting room doors on June 26, one of the Central Committee members—some say it was Khrushchev—pulled out a gun and shot Beria right then and there.

It wasn't long after Beria's execution had been announced that the party, through its press, mounted a propaganda campaign against Stalin's security chief. The charge that Beria had been a foreign spy became more specific: it was said that he was in the pay of the British for years. This is highly unlikely. Most everyone in the state security apparatus of the Soviet Union who has been shot has been accused of being a foreign, often a British, spy.

But there were true stories about Beria that were released—tales of depravity that were long known in the higher circles of the ruling elite but never spoken aloud. It seems that Beria was a sadist who would cruise the streets of Moscow in his limousine with his henchmen and abduct teenage girls. He would take them back to his house, imprisoning them in his basement. These last revelations probably came as no surprise to most of the Soviet population that suffered under the terror of Stalin and Beria.

Beria was not the only one to die. After he was killed there was a large-scale purge of the organs. The GRU/organs rivalry continued—many key figures of the organs were tortured and killed in the GRU cellars on Gogol Boulevard in Moscow.

Malenkov and Khrushchev—with Molotov fading more and more into the background—seized control of the country. Although Khrushchev would eventually emerge as the sole leader, his wasn't a brutal Stalinist grab for power. Georgi Malenkov lived out his years in a position of some importance, dying in the fall of 1987.

In those first few months after the deaths of Stalin and Beria, Khrushchev, Malenkov, and the other party leaders strove to restructure the system so that a Stalin could never again be a possibility. Even more of a threat, they felt, was the amount of power Beria alone had. That, they felt, should never happen again either.

To head the organs they turned to Sergei Kruglov, the man Stalin had employed to watch Beria, and the man who Beria ousted as head of the MVD as soon as he could after Stalin died. Kruglov's job was to reorganize the organs so that no chief would ever again have the singular power that had been Beria's. He was also instructed to clean the organs of all of Beria's cronies and appointees, often replacing them with men who had been cast aside by Stalin and Beria.

There was one thing that Beria had done with the organs that Kruglov did not change. In the weeks following Stalin's death, Beria had brought the MVD—Ministry for Internal Affairs—and the MGB—the Ministry for State Security—back together into one agency, as they had been in the 1930s when the NKVD ran both internal affairs and state security operations.

The renewed organs were given a new name that implicitly marked its demotion. The organs' status changed from that of a ministry to that of commissariat. The new name for the organs was the Committee for State Security, in Russian the Komitet Gosudarstvennoy Bezopastnosti, or KGB.

5.

THE COLD WAR AND THE KGB

While all the political intrigues, plots, and maneuvers were being played out in the Soviet Union, the Soviet Union itself was involved in larger scale political intrigues, plots and maneuvers in the world at large.

The end of World War II marked the beginning of a radically new era for the Soviet Union on the international scene. There had been something distinctly insular and almost isolationist about the first three decades of Soviet Russia; the country was cut off to a degree from the doings of other nations both because it didn't want much to do with the capitalist countries and because those countries didn't want to deal with communists. World War II changed that. When the Soviet Union, belatedly, joined the Allies, it became a true world power.

That stature grew and changed after the war. The Soviet Union quickly rose to a new level of international power in 1949 when it detonated its first atomic bomb, and it cemented that position a few years later when it set off its first hydrogen bomb. Becoming a nuclear power elevated the Soviet Union to the status of a superpower. However, the Soviet Union isn't a superpower simply because it has nuclear weapons—Britain and France (and most likely India, Israel, and South Africa) have nuclear weapons, but they are not superpowers. That status also has to do with conventional military might and economic and political influence around the world.

The Soviets, despite all their early aims at worldwide revolution, hadn't ventured far beyond their borders until that point. They had tried to export revolution in the past (the failed German revolution in the early 1920s most notably), and they had tried to grab land from others (the failed invasion of Finland in the 1930s), but they had been unsuccessful. They had been successful at subjugating the various states that they felt fell within the purview of the Union (including Armenia, Estonia, Latvia, the Ukraine and several others), but their efforts beyond that border yielded little. At the Yalta and Potsdam conferences of the leaders of the three most powerful Allied nations (the United States, Britain and the USSR), however, the Soviet Union was given the freedom to exert its influence over a string of countries along its western border. Domination over these countries in Eastern Europe—Hungary, Poland, Czechoslovakia, Romania, Bulgaria, and East Germany—marked the first true successful expansion of Soviet influence and power. Since then, the Soviets have been off and running.

Of course the Soviet Union was not alone in those postwar years in its efforts to expand its power and influence around the world; there was also the United States. Like the Soviet Union, the United States had been moderately isolationist until World War II (there was a strong contingent within the United States that didn't even want to get involved in that conflict, saying that it was Europe's concern and not America's) and then began rapidly to spread its influence around the globe after the war. These two countries, which had been allies during the war, quickly became the staunchest of enemies.

Despite all the finger-pointing and name-calling (the Soviets calling Americans "imperialist warmongers" and President Reagan calling the Soviet Union the "Evil Empire"), the foreign policy goals of these two nations have been similar in a way. Both have sought to gain economic and political control around the world. The ideologies of these two nations, of course, are not the same. Much of the conflict between the United States and the Soviet Union has been ideological—democracy vs. totalitarianism, capitalism vs. communism. But it is also true that much of the conflict has been expansionism vs. expansionism. And, of course, both sides blame the other and say that their own efforts abroad come only in response to their enemy's—"we are only expanding to thwart their expansion."

The central conflict, then, of the post-World War II years has been the struggle between the superpowers, the United States and the Soviet Union. They have not fought each other directly, primarily because with nuclear weapons they cannot afford to. With thousands upon thousands of nuclear warheads aimed at each other, any head-to-head battle would obliterate both sides and most likely all life on the planet. So, the conflict has been carried out in other ways, usually in other nations—the US can't fight the Soviets directly, so it arms rebels to harass them in Soviet-held Afghanistan; the Soviets won't assault America's security interests in Israel directly, but it does back terrorists who seek to bring down the Israeli state.

This long-term conflict between the United States and the Soviet Union has been a war of sorts—a war of ideologies, a war of words, a war fought through third parties—but it has not involved any large-scale direct battles. For that reason, it was, many years ago, dubbed the "Cold War," as opposed to a hot war, which would involve the firing of guns and the launching of missiles. As the postwar years have been singularly characterized by the US-USSR conflict, so the entire period can be thought of as the Cold War era. But this has not been one large, unchanging, undifferentiated time in history; there have been distinct eras within the larger era of the Cold War.

A BRIEF HISTORY OF THE COLD WAR

The Cold War has changed and evolved over the years in part as the Soviet and American leadership has changed.

There was a certain amount of chaos and upheaval in world affairs when Harry S. Truman was president and Stalin continued in power. In those years, from the end of the war into the early part of the 1950s, the Cold War was just beginning and no one really knew what it was going to be like, or how it would be fought, or who would win it. There was perhaps a greater sense of urgency then, as if the future of the world would be decided in a short time. Few thought the simmering conflict would continue without a major catastrophe in the decades to come.

A typical US-USSR conflict of the time came during the Italian elections of 1948. The US, through the Central Intelligence Agency, poured millions of dollars into an effort to stop the Italian communist party—undoubtedly receiving support, however circuitously obtained, from the Soviets—from coming to power. The United States won. However, when the US tried to foment anticommunism in Eastern Europe (notably in Albania and Poland) the US lost and the Soviets won. Such struggles as these, carried out by diplomats and spies, were completely clandestine.

Within the space of a few years Stalin died and Khrushchev came to power in the Soviet Union and Dwight D. Eisenhower, a Republican (and former commander of the Allied Forces during World War II), was elected president in the United States. During the Eisenhower-Khrushchev years, the rivalry between the United States and the Soviet Union gained the preeminence in world affairs that it continues to have to this day. As the Cold War began to take shape it was waged on several fronts.

The US had given up on the idea of changing things in the Soviet Union or Eastern Europe so it looked elsewhere, to countries in the Third World that seemed to teeter between siding with the Soviets or remaining loyal to the United States. So, whenever it seemed like a country was shifting to the left, the US—usually through the CIA—stepped in. In particular in the mid-1950s, the CIA was responsible for the overthrow of governments in Guatemala and Iran that it perceived to be sympathetic to the communists.

At the same time, the Soviets continued to back any and all revolutionary movements around the world. This wasn't done solely for ideological reasons. As the US had the strongest connections with those already in power, the only way for the Soviets to subvert that hold was to back those who were on the outside who might someday come to power.

The Cold War was also fought on a technological front, the primary concern being nuclear and missile capability. This was the era of the "gaps." The Soviets proudly unveiled a new bomber during the May Day parade in 1954 and it seemed as if there was a bomber gap—that the Soviets had a faster bomber than the US, and more of them. Later, Khrushchev bragged about the Soviet missile arsenal and it seemed as if there was a missile gap. These gaps were only closed when the US spyplane, the U-2, finally got a look at what was going on inside secrecy-shrouded Russia and discovered that the Soviets had far fewer bombers and missiles than had been feared and that if there were any gaps they were in favor of the United States.

The United States' major battle with communism in this period was played out in a very hot war—the Korean War. Communist North Korea, with backing from China, invaded South Korea, and United Nations troops (primarily Americans) helped the South defend itself. When the forces from the North were pushed back and were threatened with total defeat, China sent in its own troops. The conflict settled into a stalemate and Korea remains divided into communist North and US-backed South.

The Soviets' major battle in that period came in one of its satellite nations, Hungary, which, in 1956, had the audacity to stake a claim to some measure of independence and tried to institute some reforms. The Soviets quickly moved in and crushed the dissent.

While Khrushchev remained in power, in the United States in 1960, there was a change of administration and John F. Kennedy was elected president. In his few short years in the presidency Kennedy would have more head-to-head run-ins with the Soviets than any other president. The first major conflict began before he was elected and lasted until the fall of 1961. It had to do with the fate of Berlin, a city divided—one side belonging to communist East Germany, the other to democratic West Germany. At this point the fiction of the missile gap still survived, and Khrushchev attempted to press his presumed advantage and sought to have Berlin united under East German control. This became a major crisis, one that even threatened nuclear war in Europe. Khrushchev backed off in the fall of 1961 when the United States privately showed the Soviets spy satellite photos that proved that they knew the Soviets didn't have as many missiles as they said they did.

An even more frightening crisis occurred in the fall of 1962 when the Soviets started to place nuclear missiles on the island of Cuba. Cuba had been pro-American until 1959 when Fidel Castro and his revolutionary army of guerrillas overthrew the corrupt government of Fulgencio Batista. Although Castro's revolution had not been backed by the Soviets, he quickly turned to them for support (the United States refused to recognize or support his new government). Eager to have a base of operations so close to the United States, the Soviets poured vast amounts of money and military equipment into Cuba. In the summer of 1962, this equipment began to include missiles and nuclear warheads. When the United States discovered this (it was confirmed by spy plane flights), Kennedy told the Soviets to move the missiles out or Cuba would be invaded. Such an invasion would likely have triggered a nuclear war. For two weeks in October 1962, the world held its breath. Finally, Khrushchev backed down and agreed to remove the missiles.

Strangely, this crisis with nearly catastrophic consequences was good for East-West relations—Kennedy and Khrushchev developed a "special relationship" and things cooled off for a while. After Kennedy's assassination in November 1963 and Khrushchev's ouster in 1964, however, the Cold War heated up again. The primary field of battle between the United States and communism for the rest of

An aerial photo of a missile site in Cuba, taken by a U-2 spy plane during the height of the Cuban missile crisis in October 1962. [Credit: U.S. Air Force]

the 1960s, through all of Lyndon Johnson's presidency and most of Richard Nixon's, was Vietnam.

Throughout the 1960s the Soviets' policy of backing revolutionary groups around the world began to bear fruit, as US-backed governments fell and pro-Soviet people came to power. The Soviets had been backing the communist forces in Vietnam led by Ho Chi Minh since the late 1940s. They intensified their support as Ho Chi Minh consolidated his power and the country was divided into a communist North and a US-backed South in 1954. The conflict between the two halves of the country simmered for 10 years, then escalated into a full-scale civil war between North and South in 1965, when the United States sent in troops to support the South. This conflict—the most unpopular and divisive war

Afghani rebels shown atop a captured Soviet tank in 1980. The KGB was in Afghanistan before the tanks rolled in in 1979 and will remain after the tanks roll out. [Credit: UPI/Bettmann Newsphotos]

in United States history—dragged on for eight years. In 1973 the United States pulled its last troops out; the South quickly collapsed; and by 1975 the communists had assumed complete control of the entire country.

The leader of the Soviet Union in this period was Leonid Brezhnev. Through high-level summits and negotiations with United States President Nixon, the Cold War entered the era of *détente*. The idea was for the US and USSR to peacefully coexist, with neither attempting to change or defeat the other, with neither expanding their spheres of influence. Détente seemed to work—at least on the surface. While it did produce several nuclear-weapons treaties, both sides continued to try to outmaneuver the other around the world; the Soviets still backed revolutionary movements in Africa and the United States aided in the overthrow of the democratically elected Marxist government in Chile.

Jimmy Carter inherited détente when he was elected president in 1976 and he sought to keep it alive. It came crashing down, however, in December 1979 when Soviet troops invaded Afghanistan. It was further crushed in the early 1980s when the Soviets pressured the Polish government to crack down on the Solidarity trade union movement that the Soviets viewed as a threat to their totalitarian control of Eastern Europe.

Ronald Reagan was president of the United States for most of the 1980s, while in the Soviet Union there was a succession of leaders as Brezhnev died and was succeeded by KGB-chief Yuri Andropov, who died and was followed by the ailing Konstantin Chernenko. Chernenko died and was succeeded by Mikhail Gorbachev.

For much of Reagan's two terms as president, relations between the two countries were again acrimonious. The two major battlefields of the Cold War in this era were the Middle East, where both sides continued to vie for influence and control (with the United States supporting Israel and the moderate Arab nations, and the Soviets backing the Palestine Liberation Organization and anti-Israeli Arab nations) and Central America. In Central America the Soviets and Cubans aided the various revolutionary movements and supported the socialist Sandinista government in Nicaragua that overthrew the corrupt and oppressive Somoza regime in 1979. The United States backed the contras who were fighting against the Sandinistas.

In 1986, Gorbachev began to institute reforms in the Soviet Union under a new policy of openness, called *glasnost*. This has certainly helped ease the friction between the superpowers. Whether Gorbachev will succeed in his goals is uncertain. As well, it is far too early to tell what the effect of the election of George Bush to the presidency will have on the Cold War.

Now, where does the KGB fit into all of this? Everywhere.

We discussed earlier how the three most powerful institutions in the Soviet Union are the party, the military, and the organs. When it comes to engaging in the Cold War, the organs take center stage. The Soviet Union has a diplomatic service and its version of the State Department, but in truth its diplomatic mission is subservient to the organs. Most Soviet diplomats, trade representatives, and the like are KGB agents, or report to the KGB. In the world of foreign affairs, the KGB is the Soviet Union's dominant instrument.

While the KGB has played a role in every major facet of the Cold War, its involvement has been more important in some areas than in others. For example, while the KGB has undoubtably been active in Afghanistan, that conflict can still be characterized as a military mission. On the other hand, the KGB was without a doubt the most important player in crushing the uprising in Hungary in 1956, even though the Red Army's troops and tanks did the actual crushing.

The KGB has fought the Cold War on many fronts these past four decades. The main areas of concern for the Soviets during the Cold War have been reining in dissent at home, suppressing nationalism in the various republics, controlling the satellite countries in Eastern Europe, expanding its power and influence in the Middle East and the Third World, and penetrating the West to gain its secrets and influence its course of action. On each of these fronts there is something different at stake for the Soviets—in some cases what is at stake is something they could lose; in other cases it's what they could win.

We will now take a second look at the Cold War, this time specifically in terms of the KGB—what its goals have been and what it has accomplished, in three particular and vital areas: at home, in the satellite nations of Eastern Europe, and in the West.

SUPPRESSING NATIONALISM

As mentioned earlier in the book, the Soviet Union is not entirely synonymous with Russia. While Russia (including Siberia) is the largest republic within the Union of Soviet Socialist Republics, there are fourteen other republics. They include the Ukraine, Latvia, Estonia (in the west), Georgia, and Armenia (in the south) and the various republics of Central Asia. In many of these republics there is a fierce nationalist sentiment, and the people are not particularly happy to be living under the control of Moscow.

This nationalism is something that has always concerned Moscow. In the first decade of the Cold War, this suppression of nationalism was carried out by the KGB using the most despicable methods, including assassination, even if it meant going outside of the USSR.

In 1957 the KGB targeted Lev Rebet, an influential Ukrainian émigré living in West Germany. Rebet was working for the independence of the Ukraine; as far as the KGB was concerned, this was grounds for his assassination. The job was given to a young agent, 25 year-old Bogdan Stashinsky. A Ukrainian himself, Stashinsky had been in training with the organs since he was 19, and this was his first assignment, given to him as something of a entrance test that he had to pass before he could enter the KGB's elite club that carried out *mokrie dela*—"wet work." With this club, however, if an agent fails to gain admittance, he is most likely killed.

To murder Rebet, Stashinsky was given a pistol contraption loaded with a small capsule of prussic acid. He was to fire the pistol in Rebet's face. Rebet would inhale the prussic acid dust, which would enter his lungs and bloodstream and trigger a fatal heart attack that would appear natural in an autopsy. Stashinsky was given an antidote that he was to take before and after firing the pistol. He was assured that the antidote would prevent him from suffering the same fate as Rebet. Although he was unsure if the antidote would work, he was certain he would be killed if he didn't carry out the assignment. He killed Rebet on October 12, 1957. He was now in the club, but he was not happy about it.

The next assignment for Stashinsky was to kill Stefan Bandera, another exiled Ukrainian leader. Because Bandera rarely went anywhere without his bodyguard, Stashinsky was given a double-barreled prussic acid pistol so he could kill both men at once (how the KGB thought two men having simultaneous heart attacks would appear natural is unclear). Stashinsky did not feel good about this and lost his nerve in the first attempt to kill Bandera. He had plausible excuses but his superiors were not pleased and pushed him on. Stashinsky gave in to the pressure and on October 15, 1959, found Bandera alone and killed him.

In December 1959, Stashinsky was awarded the Order of the Red Banner by KGB chief Shelepin for carrying out an "important government commission." On August 12, 1961, plagued by a sense of guilt and remorse for his actions, Stashinsky and his wife slipped into West Berlin and Stashinsky gave himself up to police. He confessed to the murders, was put on trial, and, in light of the fact that he had been acting under the orders of his government and had fled his country to turn himself in, was given a relatively light sentence of eight years.

The Soviets continue to be worried about nationalism in the republics. Even current Soviet leader Mikhail Gorbachev, who touts reforms and relaxations in many areas of Soviet government, felt it necessary to crack down on the nationalism expressed in Armenia in 1987 and 1988. (The Armenians were petitioning to have a section of a neighboring republic, inhabited primarily by ethnic Armenians, brought into Armenia; it was not allowed.) While the KGB didn't send in assassins to curb the recent surge of nationalism in Armenia, they were undoubtably there, nonetheless, working to coerce local party officials into towing the Moscow line and infiltrating the ranks of those who the Kremlin regarded as troublesome.

THE SATELLITES AND THE BROTHERS

If the Soviets are worried about nationalism in their republics, they are terrified of any murmurs of independence in their satellite countries in the Eastern bloc. To "lose" one of these countries, to have it slide out from under the control of Moscow, would be a catastrophe to the Soviets, for if one were to go, perhaps they all would and that would threaten the stability of the Soviet government itself. The events of 1956 in Hungary show how the Soviets react to any attempt by a satellite country to throw off the yoke of the USSR, and they show how enforcing the will of the Kremlin is the job of the KGB. A look at the events that occurred in Hungary in 1956 will also introduce us to one of the most important figures in the history of the organs—Yuri Andropov.

Andropov was born in Russia on June 15, 1914. In his early years he was headed into a technical field; he worked as a telegraph operator, an apprentice movie projectionist, and then entered the Technical School of Water Transportation in Rybinsk. He became an organizer for Komsomol—the communist party youth organization. It was during World War II that he had his first taste of secret intelligence work, fighting with the partisans behind German lines.

Andropov began to make his mark in 1954 when he was sent to Hungary by the KGB as a counsellor—a mid-level

Yuri Andropov. This picture was released by the Soviets in 1967 when Andropov was appointed chief of the KGB. In 1982, Andropov succeeded Brezhnev as leader of the Soviet Union, becoming the first head of the organs to rise to the leadership of the nation. [Credit: UPI/Bettmann Newsphotos]

KGB officer. He soon had the responsibilities of KGB resident—the chief KGB officer—in Budapest, the capital of Hungary. Although in theory the KGB was just supposed to advise the Hungarian secret police, the AVH, in practice, Andropov controlled it. But he first had to get his own house in order. The KGB was in disarray in Hungary and

Andropov quickly reorganized it, removing all the old officers; bringing in fresh agents from Moscow. But Andropov was faced with larger problems in Hungary—the country was about to erupt.

The leader of the Hungarian communist party at that time was Imre Nagy. Nagy had the radical—and, as far as the Soviet Politburo was concerned, disquieting—notion that the Hungarian people deserved some measure of freedom and happiness. Soviet leaders Khrushchev and Malenkov were afraid that this indicated that the Soviet empire was weak in Hungary. It was Andropov's job to correct that.

Andropov acted decisively. He had KGB and AVH agents infiltrate the groups of protesters and dissenters. Then, he went straight to the top and ordered Nagy to step down as leader of the country on April 18, 1955. Nagy had no choice but to agree. Andropov then brought in a party hack he could control, Erno Gero.

It was about this time that Andropov was made ambassador to Hungary. He still worked for the KGB, but this promotion gave him a more official capacity. It was as ambassador to Hungary that Andropov first began to make his reputation in diplomatic circles. He was tall, well mannered, articulate, and came off as intelligent, sophisticated, and urbane. Unlike Soviet ambassadors in Budapest before him, he took the trouble to learn Hungarian. And he even showed a sense of humor every now and then.

Putting Gero in power didn't work out. The people were still clamoring for reforms and the Hungarian communist party wanted Nagy back. Andropov bowed to their wishes and said that Nagy would return to the leadership on October 23, 1956. That was never to be. Before Nagy could return, a full-scale uprising broke out when AVH officers opened fire on a crowd. Gero was still in power at the time. He asked the Soviets—no doubt after being "advised" by Andropov—to send in troops to quell the disturbances. The response was swift and the country quieted. Nagy was partly responsible for the calm—on October 18 he assured his people that the troops would leave. They did begin to pull out.

It was then that Nagy made the bold, if ultimately unwise, move of announcing that he would withdraw Hungary from the Warsaw Pact (the treaty that binds the Soviet bloc militarily). This was a slap in the face that he knew the Soviets would not stand for, but he counted on the UN and NATO to support him and step in to guarantee Hungary's independence. They didn't. Instead, the withdrawing Soviet troops turned around, were joined by reinforcements, and marched back into Hungary. The protesters didn't give up immediately—surely, they thought, the UN and NATO must come to their aid. But no one did come to their aid and they were no match for 250,000 Soviet troops and 2,500 tanks. All told, from between 6,500 to 32,000 Hungarians lost their lives in the abortive revolt.

There is some speculation that Andropov may have ordered the AVH to fire on the crowd, knowing that this would spark a revolt that would then provide the excuse needed for the invasion of Soviet troops and the harsh clampdown that followed.

Thousands of people fled the country and Andropov made use of that. Instead of trying to stop all of them, he planted many KGB and AVH agents into the middle of the exodus so that they could then spy in the Western nations that received them.

When Beria was brought down as the head of the organs, the excuse used was an abortive uprising in East Germany. Before and since, East Germany has been a particular worry of the organs. One operation in East Germany in 1952 shows how the KGB wasn't just involved in large-scale operations as in the case of Hungary, but that they would also work on a smaller scale to suppress independence in the satellite countries.

On July 8, 1952, Dr. Walter Linse, head of the Association of Free German Jurists—a group that was fighting the division of Germany into East and West—stepped out of his home in Berlin. A man approached him and asked him for a match. As Linse reached into his pocket, another man clubbed him from behind. The two men then struggled to push Linse into a car. Linse fought back, so one of the men shot him in the leg, pushed him inside the car, then drove off. Police took up the pursuit. The car containing Linse entered the Soviet sector, but as soon as it passed through the barricade, the barrier came down, preventing the police from following. Linse was never seen in the West again.

Initially the Soviets denied all knowledge of Linse's whereabouts, although there were reports from people who escaped from the Soviet Union that Linse had been spotted in a labor camp in the mid-50s. Years later the Soviets finally admitted that Linse had been in their country, but said that he had died in 1953.

A bust of Stalin is tumbled onto a Budapest street and annointed with a traffic sign during the ill-fated Hungarian uprising in the fall of 1956. [Credit: UPI/Bettmann Newsphotos]

Over the years, the Soviets have had other run-ins with those in the satellite countries that might seek some measure of independence from Moscow. In 1948, Jan Masaryk, the Czech foreign minister at the time, made the fatal mistake of suggesting that Czechoslovakia should be neutral in the Cold War and free from Soviet influence. He was assassinated by the organs for the error of his ways. In 1968 Czechoslovakia again became a problem when Czech leader Dubcek tried to institute reforms, to create communism "with a human face" as it was put at that time. That period in Czechoslovakia became known as the "Prague Spring." (Prague is the capital of Czechoslovakia.) Spring didn't last long. In the summer Soviet tanks rolled in to smother the breath of freedom. The Czechs, having learned of the futility of fighting back from the experience of the Hungarians in '56, put up little resistance and there was nowhere near the bloodshed that had occurred in Budapest 12 years before.

In recent years, the Soviets have had to contend with the Solidarity trade union movement in Poland led by Lech Walesa. In 1982 the Soviets didn't send in tanks, but they did arrange a change of leadership in Poland—putting a military man, General Jaruzelski, in charge—and had Solidarity outlawed. The trade union movement went underground, making a big comeback in 1988, causing yet another crisis for Polish and Soviet authorities. The KGB's involvement in Czechoslovakia in 1968 and Poland now is probably no different than its involvement in Hungary in1956—infiltrating the ranks of the dissenters and using the Czech and Polish secret police to do its bidding.

It's important to realize how directly and completely the KGB controls the secret police of the countries under its influence.

The Knights of the Cross Monastery in Prague, Czechoslovakia, was once one of the most important Christian churches in Czechoslovakia. Since 1961 it has been the home of the State Secret Security of Czechoslovakia—the Statni

Tajna Bezpecnost, the STB. The STB is the Czech equivalent of the KGB. To the KGB it is a "brother."

The KGB has many brothers. The state secret security organizations of all the Soviet bloc countries are at the beck and call of the KGB. The UB in Poland, Hungary's AVH, the East German SSD, the Czech STB, and the DGI in Cuba—as well as smaller agencies in Romania, Bulgaria, and elsewhere—will all do the bidding of their "elders" in Moscow.

It's not simply that the KGB influences the brothers; it actually maintains a rather firm, hands-on control of their day-to-day actions. The relationship is analogous to that between the head office of a multinational corporation and its subsidiaries around the world; the individual companies may have some autonomy, but in the final analysis, headquarters calls the shots.

The organs began using agents of the brothers as early as 1946. At that time they were primarily used in "wet work." Later on, the organs helped the Soviet bloc countries create their own security police in the image of the organs. When Ivan Alexandrovich Serov took over as the head of the KGB in 1954 he was faced with the prospect of running a seriously depleted and ill-working intelligence service. Hamstrung by Khrushchev and the Politburo, one of Serov's only options was to use the brothers as much as possible. From that time on, the KGB has been thoroughly enmeshed in the affairs of the brothers.

In the early days of this relationship, the KGB officers sent to supervise the work of the brothers were characteristically intimidating thugs. From the early 1960s on, the KGB opted for a more polite and cooperative approach, while at the same time not relaxing its control an iota. For example, at the STB, no major operations are conducted without KGB approval, and an STB officer will often first submit a proposal to the resident KGB "uncle" to see what he thinks before giving it to his STB boss, as his boss's approval means nothing without the KGB's nod.

The KGB will give the brothers any number of assignments that it, for one reason or another, doesn't want to handle itself. In 1962, when a Hungarian defector fled to Austria, the KGB had the STB send in their ace agent—known, rather melodramatically, as Agent Seven—to kill the defector with an exotic poison; the mission was a success. In 1964, in an effort to disrupt the American presidential elections, the STB—on KGB orders—mounted a disinformation campaign against Republican candidate Barry Goldwater that involved distributing bogus campaign literature, supposedly written by Goldwater, that made him out to look like an utterly despicable racist.

In the 1960s, the KGB gave the East German security service, the SSD, a long-term assignment that it most successfully accomplished. They wanted the SSD to penetrate NATO—the North Atlantic Treaty Organization, which links together the United States and many of the Western European nations into one military organization. The KGB felt that the SSD could work through West Germany.

The SSD came up with a plan. Then German Chancellor Konrad Adenauer was on his way out and Berlin Mayor Willy Brandt looked like the best bet to replace him. The idea was to get someone into Brandt's camp early; someone who could then follow Brandt to the top of the West German government.

During the war, Brandt had been sheltered and attended to by a doctor who was now living in East Germany. The doctor's son, Gunther Guillaume, was a disillusioned young man who resented the presence of the Allies in Germany. He was an almost ideal recruit—politically correct and the son of a man to whom Brandt owed a debt. He got a job on Brandt's staff as an assistant.

It took some time for Brandt to fulfill expectations and become chancellor, but when he did, the hard-working and dedicated Gunther went with him. As a key assistant to the leader of West Germany, Gunther knew where all the NATO secrets were kept. Gunther didn't gather intelligence him-

Harold "Kim" Philby, the most notorious and successful (for the Soviets) of the spies recruited at Cambridge University in the 1930s. He was at one time the liaison between British and American intelligence. Although he escaped arrest, he finally fled to Moscow in 1963, where he was received as a hero. He died there in 1988. [Credit: UPI/Bettmann Newsphotos]

self—that would have been too risky for such a highly placed and valuable agent— instead, he pointed out to the SSD where the secrets were kept and who, of those that had access to them, might be recruitable as spies. Gunther's spy ring caused untold, immeasurable damage to NATO security in the late 1960s and early 1970s.

The spy ring was finally broken and Gunther arrested in 1974. Later, he and his wife were traded for West Germans that the SSD was holding. Gunther now reportedly teaches at a KGB spy school.

The KGB uses the agents of the brothers for recruitment of spies. For many people around the world, the idea of spying for the Russians may seem reprehensible, while doing some work for the Poles or the Hungarians doesn't seem so bad. Of course, anyone who spies for the Poles, Hungarians, East Germans, or Czechs is in fact spying for the KGB.

PENETRATING THE WEST

The KGB's concerns with nationalism in the Soviet republics and independence in the satellite countries are for the most part concerns of security—the fear of losing control. The KGB is also concerned with violating the security of other nations, in gaining their secrets. Their attempts to penetrate the West have resulted in several explosive spy scandals over the past 40 years.

In June 1962, a Khrushchev letter was quoted on a Radio Moscow English-language broadcast (quoted here from *KGB* by John Barron): "Espionage is needed by those who prepare for attack, for aggression. The Soviet Union is deeply dedicated to the cause of peace and does not intend to attack anyone. Therefore, it has no intention of engaging in espionage." This was an absurdity, of course. By 1962 several important Soviet spies had been uncovered around the world and there were many more to come.

In the 1930s, the OGPU, and later the NKVD, had recruited and cultivated a small group of young, communist-leaning intellectuals at prestigious Cambridge University in England. They were Guy Burgess, Donald Maclean, Harold "Kim" Philby, and Anthony Blunt. Blunt, older than the others, was the senior spy, spotting potential recruits for the Soviets.

During World War II, the three younger spies—Philby, Burgess, and Maclean—established good war records, rising high in military and diplomatic circles. They undoubtedly passed on some information to the Soviets, but they weren't to do their highest-level spying until after the war. Burgess, a severe alcoholic, never rose to the level that the Soviets had hoped, but Philby and Maclean surpassed expectations. Having been educated at Cambridge, and with impeccable backgrounds, Philby and Maclean were the sons of privilege and were admitted into the elite: an elite that they privately scorned.

Maclean secured a posting as first secretary at the British Embassy in Washington, and also got a spot on the joint commission studying atomic energy, which enabled him to pass on some vital atom bomb secrets to the Russians. Philby entered the field of intelligence and became liaison officer between the British secret service and the CIA. From this position he was able to betray agents and missions around the world.

By 1951 there were those in the CIA who were suspicious of Philby and Maclean, Maclean in particular. Maclean was withdrawn to London, but before the net closed around him, Philby tipped him off. Plans were made for his escape, but the drunken Burgess threatened to wreck it if he couldn't go with Maclean. Reluctantly, Maclean gave in. He and Burgess set off on what was supposed to be a short trip to the Continent, but turned up instead in Moscow.

Attention was then focused on Philby, but despite endless interrogations they could pin nothing on him. Part of the problem was that his interrogators, fellow members of Britain's upper class, simply couldn't believe that Philby could be involved in such treason. Philby was allowed to remain with British intelligence, although he was recalled from Washington and a cloud of suspicion remained over his head. He never again had high-level access, and, in 1963, finally defected to Moscow.

While Burgess and Maclean lived dismal lives in the Soviet Union, Philby was something of a celebrity, and he became an important advisor to KGB Chairman Yuri Andropov in the 1970s. Philby died in Moscow on May 11, 1988, at the age of 76.

George Blake, Soviet spy. This photo was released when Blake escaped from prison in England in October 1966. He eluded detection and made his way safely to the Soviet Union. [Credit: UPI/Bettmann Newsphotos]

Another famous Soviet spy in Britain was George Blake. Blake was born in Rotterdam, Holland, in 1922. As a teenager he fought with the Dutch resistance against the Nazis, then escaped to Britain. In Britain he joined the Navy. His linguistic ability brought him to the attention of the secret service. Now working for British intelligence, he was eventually sent to Berlin with orders to hook up with the Soviets and become a double agent. He did that. The trouble was he worked more for the Soviets than he did for the British. Blake hated fascism; afraid that the United States and Britain were rearming Germany, he converted to communism.

One of Blake's most damaging betrayals was his informing the Soviets of the tunnel that American intelligence had built into East Berlin for spying. Blake told the Soviets about the tunnel in 1953 but the Soviets didn't let on that they knew about it until 1956—for three years they used the tunnel to feed false intelligence to the Americans.

Blake was finally caught through a series of events triggered by the defection of a Polish intelligence officer. He was arrested in London in 1961 and sent to Wormwood Scrubs, Britain's high-security prison, with a 42-year sentence. On October 22, 1966, Blake escaped from prison. While a huge manhunt scoured the land for him, Blake simply laid low for a while then quietly slipped out of the country, eventually turning up in Moscow.

One of the most notorious Soviet spies in the United States in these years was Colonel Rudolf Abel. Abel worked out of New York City as the spymaster for a vast web of Russian spies in America. He had come in through Canada and had set up shop in Brooklyn as Emil Goldfus, an artist. In the Soviet spy pantheon he is respected on the same level as Richard Sorge. He was eventually betrayed by an assistant, a drinker, who Abel had sent back to Moscow for sloppy work. Being recalled to Moscow meant possible execution in those days, so, en route to Moscow, the assistant defected. Abel got wind of the defection and fled to Florida, where he

Colonel Rudolph Abel, Soviet master spy who ran a network of agents in New York in the 1950s. After his arrest and conviction, he was exchanged in a spy swap for Gary Powers, the downed U-2 spy plane pilot. [Credit: UPI/Bettmann Newsphotos]

hid out for some time. His superiors—mistakenly—told him that all was clear and that he should return to New York. All was not clear. Abel was tracked down and captured. He was jailed in 1957 and sentenced to 30 years. He was later exchanged at the Berlin Wall for Francis Gary Powers, the pilot of the American U-2 spy plane that had been shot down over the Soviet Union in May 1960.

One other equally famous spy, Gordon Lonsdale, was a student and operative of Abel's. Like Abel, Lonsdale was an illegal, but putting him in place was a far more elaborate affair than putting Abel in place, and it began early.

At the age of 11, Konon Trofimovich Molody, was taken to the United States by his aunt, who was posing as his mother. He used the identity of a Canadian boy, Gordon Lonsdale. Until 1938, Molody/Lonsdale attended a private school near Berkeley, California. He then returned to Moscow, where his spy training and education really began in earnest. He came back to the United States, still under the Lonsdale identity, in the 1950s. He worked under Abel and became something of a protégé. In 1955, Abel pulled some strings and arranged for Lonsdale to be posted to Britain as the Resident Director.

Gordon Lonsdale quickly established himself as an "English gentleman" and something of a womanizer. But he was also the consummate professional and he set out aggressively to recruit agents. His target was NATO and his cover was that of owner of a jukebox rental company. That cover allowed him admission to every military base with a jukebox.

Two of Lonsdale's key spies were Morris and Lona Cohen, posing as Peter and Helen Kroger. They lived in a bungalow in Middlesex that Lonsdale had equipped with all the necessary spy equipment, including a radio transmitter, plans concealed in a butane lighter, and a microdot reader hidden in a tin of talcum powder.

Lonsdale's operation fell apart when he recruited a Navy clerk working in Underwater Weapons research. Recruiting the man was no problem—Lonsdale simply posed as an American agent, saying that friendly countries spy on each other all the time (as they do), reassuring the clerk that it was no big deal. Trouble arose because Lonsdale paid the man too much. The clerk's sudden surfeit of cash caught the attention of his superiors who took a closer look. The whole operation caved in. Lonsdale was eventually exchanged in a spy swap—in October 1970—for Greville Wynne, the British businessman who had been the contact for a Soviet GRU officer, Oleg Penkovsky, who had been spying for the West. (More on him later.)

There were numerous other spy scandals involving Soviet agents around the world in the 1950s and 1960s. These were the years of the true spy vs. spy intrigues that have filled so much of espionage fiction. In Vienna, there were poisonings and spies throwing rival spies out of trains. Much of the Soviet spy effort was concentrated in Berlin, and, as in the case of the abduction of Linse, there were occasions of car chases in the streets. The Soviets had spy rings around the world in these years. There was a major ring, run out of Italy, that spanned from Scandinavia to North Africa. At the head of the ring were Giorgio Rinaldi, an Italian parachutist and stuntman, and his wife, Angela Maria. The Soviets even had an agent in the Vatican—Father Aligheri Tondi, who had been planted in the Jesuit order.

All of these spy scandals made one thing perfectly clear: when Khrushchev wrote in 1962 that the Soviet Union had no intention of engaging in espionage, he must have been chuckling to himself.

In the 1970s, there was a slight change in the KGB attempts to penetrate the West. The Soviets had always been interested in stealing military-technology secrets, in the 70s this interest became dominant, and it extended beyond what one would think of immediately as military-related. The KGB became interested in all facets of American high-technology, especially computers. It's not that the Soviets couldn't develop their own high-speed computer chip, but why bother if they could save time and money by stealing the design. The KGB now has agents swarming over Silicon Valley, the area south of San Francisco where much of America's computer research and development is done.

There weren't the big, splashy spy scandals in the 1970s as there were in the 60s. This didn't mean that spying wasn't going on, just that the spies weren't being caught; and those that were caught were almost always the recruits, not the spymasters. The Soviets have always used recruits to do the actual spying, of course, but those recruits, in the past, were "run" or controlled by illegal, undercover spies. Interestingly enough, in the scandals of the past decade or so, the recruits have apparently been run by legals—KGB officers working out of an embassy or trade mission. This may reflect a change in policy for the KGB away from the use of illegals or may simply mean that the illegals are just not being caught.

The type of people recruited to spy for the KGB has also changed over the years. The KGB used to attract a certain number of ideological recruits—people who believed in the Soviet system—but not so much anymore. In the 1970s the Soviets did get one major ideological recruit—Christopher Boyce. Boyce was working for TRW, a major high-tech defense contractor in California, when he sold the Soviets secrets about an advanced American spy satellite. But, while Boyce was ideologically motivated, he was sparked not by any love of the Soviet Union but by anger over American activities. Boyce was enraged when he found out that the CIA had tried to meddle in the affairs of Australia in the early 1970s.

Boyce's partner in that spy scandal, Daunton Lee, was the more typical spy of today. He did it for the money and the excitement. Being a spy was a thrill; he got the chance to act like James Bond.

What is most interesting about the Boyce case and most of the spy scandals of the past few years is that the spies weren't even recruited—they volunteered. Like Daunton Lee, they did it for the money and the thrill.

Undoubtedly the biggest spy scandal of the past decade has been the Walker/Whitworth affair. John Walker, an ex-Navy man had the idea; his son, and a colleague, Jerry Whitworth, supplied the secrets. Between 1976 and 1985 they made hundreds of thousands of dollars selling secrets to the KGB. Whitworth's information in particular was damaging. He worked with cipher machines on the nuclear-powered aircraft carrier *Enterprise*. He gave the Soviets all they needed to know about breaking United States Navy codes: the type of information that could easily spell defeat in wartime. The KGB considers this operation—which had a much longer life than most spy operations—to be a high watermark in the history of the organs. One of the three key KGB officers who shepherded the case was awarded the Hero of the Soviet Union, and two others received the Order of the Red Banner.

Another big loss for the Americans and a big gain for the KGB was the information sold to the Soviets by Ronald Pelton in the late 1970s. Pelton had been working for the National Security Agency, the spy agency responsible for making America's secret codes and breaking those of other nations. Pelton, for money, betrayed the highly classified Ivy Bells operation, in which the NSA, with the help of the Navy, had tapped into Soviet communications cables on the bottom of the ocean.

Pelton was only caught when a KGB defector, Vitaly Yurchenko, tipped the CIA off about him in 1985. Yurchenko also tipped the CIA off about another traitor in their midst, Edward Lee Howard, a former employee who had been trained to work for the CIA in Moscow but who had been fired for petty theft before he was posted there. Howard betrayed the entire CIA operation in Moscow, leading to the execution of at least one Soviet recruit. Howard eluded the FBI and ended up in the Soviet Union. Yurchenko himself returned to the Soviet Union after having a change of heart.

The two biggest spy stories of 1987 had to do with the American embassy in Moscow. First, it was discovered that the new embassy building being constructed was riddled with bugging devices. Some incredibly sophisticated devices were built into the steel I-beams. The building has been so compromised that it may be impossible to make it secure. Although it cost over $100 million, it may never be used. Then, it was discovered that a Marine assigned to guard the embassy had been seduced by a female KGB agent into allowing her access to sensitive areas of the embassy. That simply shows that as much as spying changes, it remains the same.

Throughout the Cold War the KGB, then, has been concerned with suppressing nationalism in the Soviet republics and independence in the satellite countries, and it has been trying (often successfully) to penetrate the West. The scope of its operations around the world is far too broad to be encompassed here. Suffice it to say, whether it's Vietnam or Angola, Cuba or Nicaragua, wherever the Soviet Union is represented, the KGB is also.

It is easy to think of the KGB as a single, monolithic entity that has remained unchanged throughout the Cold War, carrying out operations as any faceless bureaucracy would, devoid of personality. That would be a mistake, for the KGB was not at all immune to the changing tides in the Soviet Union over the past 40 years. Indeed the post-Stalin years have been most turbulent for the organs.

THE NEW ORGANS

By all rights, the first chief of the newly named KGB in 1953 should have been Sergei Kruglov. Kruglov was genuinely popular not only throughout the Soviet government but in international circles as well. For his work in handling the security of the conferences at Yalta and Potsdam, he was awarded both an honorary knighthood of the British Empire by Churchill and the American Legion of

Merit by Truman. At Yalta he played the role of comic Russian bear, speaking heavily accented broken English with wild malapropisms, much to the delight of the Britons and Americans. In fact, he was perfectly fluent in English and didn't miss a word he heard. At Potsdam his comic routine extended to drawing out huge guffaws by taking an offered stick of gum and chewing it, paper, foil and all. Kruglov was anything but a fool. He was a shrewd man, and would have made a formidable organs chief. But he suffered a heart attack and never had a chance to serve as KGB chief.

Replacing him, and serving as first chief of the KGB, was Ivan Alexandrovich Serov.

Serov has the rare distinction of being the only GRU officer to ever head the KGB. KGB men are appointed to head the GRU, but usually never the other way around. Serov's career was cat-like—no matter what happened, he managed to land on his feet. When the GRU was being liquidated in 1937, Serov not only survived, he managed to transfer to the NKVD. He would back any horse he thought would be a winner. In 1951 he backed Beria in the ouster of Abakumov. In 1953 he switched sides and lent his weight, as deputy director of the GRU, to those seeking Beria's overthrow. As a reward, he was chosen to head the KGB.

Serov's career was also spattered with blood. When he jumped from the GRU to the NKVD he became an executioner, personally killing several members of the Red Army general staff. He took part in the massive killings of great numbers of Latvians, Lithuanians, and Estonians in the 1940s, and he has even been linked to the massacre of thousands of Polish officers in the Katyn forest during the war.

Serov had a difficult task lying ahead of him when he took the reins at the KGB. The organs had received what amounted to a demotion; the foreign operations were depleted and in disarray and there wasn't much of a machinery to get things going again. That's exactly what Khrushchev and the other Politburo leaders wanted. They were still shuddering over how close Beria came to seizing control of the country. They wanted the KGB hobbled and on a short leash.

Serov's tenure lasted four years. He left the KGB in 1958 because he was a Stalinist and Khrushchev wanted one of his own men in. To replace Serov, Khrushchev appointed Aleksandr Nikoloevich Shelepin. Shelepin was the first non-professional to head the organs. He had been head of Komsomol, the communist youth organization, and had absolutely no experience in running the state secret security apparatus. He was appointed as part of Khrushchev's campaign to improve the KGB's image in the eyes of the public. This wasn't just a matter of public relations. The public had become so terrified of the organs that they were reluctant to go to the KGB to tell them about anything suspicious their neighbors or coworkers might be up to. In the days of Stalin, executions were so capricious and paranoia ran so high that an informer was just as likely to be shot as the person he informed on.

There was another reason Khrushchev replaced Serov with Shelepin—he needed Serov for another task. He sent him back to his alma mater—the GRU. The GRU had gotten out of line. It had backed a Red Army general's attempt to oust Khrushchev and Serov was to be their punishment.

Serov's arrival at the GRU signaled a final blow to military intelligence's quest for independence. From that moment on, the GRU in effect became a subsidiary of the KGB. Even though the GRU's leaders have struggled for some measure of autonomy, the KGB is firmly in control of all aspects of intelligence gathering in the Soviet Union.

Another reason Serov was sent to the GRU was because of a Soviet spy scandal. In 1958 a GRU lieutenant-colonel, Yuri Popov, was discovered to be a CIA spy. Serov was sent in to clean up the place. It is ironic, then, that it was under his tenure that the GRU suffered its most grievous security failures. Serov was so hated and feared by his GRU officers—he had a reputation for being a sadist—that his tenure marked the only time that GRU officers were not only recruited by Western intelligence services, but actively volunteered.

The worst blow to Serov and the GRU came in 1962 when the KGB discovered that GRU Colonel Oleg Penkovsky was a Western agent, working for both British intelligence and the CIA. In his years as a spy, Penkovsky smuggled out vast amounts of very damaging secrets through a British businessman, Greville Wynne, who traveled to Moscow supposedly to make trade deals with the Soviets. As a chief officer in the GRU he knew everything there was to know about operations overseas, what agents the GRU and KGB had where, as well as important military secrets. It is even believed that intelligence from Penkovsky—who once worked on the Soviet missile program—helped President Kennedy during the Cuban missile crisis in the fall of 1962, when the US discovered that the Soviets were placing nuclear missiles in Cuba.

What made the Penkovsky debacle doubly embarrassing for Serov was that Penkovsky was not only a personal friend of many high-ranking GRU officers, he was, in fact, an intimate friend of Serov's daughter. Serov couldn't land on his feet this time. In 1962, the bullet that he had been dodging since the days of the Stalinist purges finally caught up with him.

Back at the KGB, the new chief, Shelepin, was surprising people. Although he was not an organs veteran, this non-professional did surprisingly well as the head of the KGB. He was a good organizer, and under him the KGB became a solid, well- functioning intelligence service. It was plagued by nepotism—the hiring and promotion of one's relatives— but it is the rare part of Soviet bureaucracy that isn't.

Shelepin's tenure as KGB chief was shaken by the CIA-sponsored invasion of Cuba at the Bay of Pigs in April 1961. Usually when an intelligence chief is brought to task over a world event it's because his staff didn't predict it. In this case, however, Shelepin had been passing along information that suggested that the Americans might invade Cuba, but he had been ignored. He was harangued, in a sense, for not making the Politburo believe him.

Oleg Penkovsky, the GRU officer who spied for Britain and the United States, is shown here in Moscow as he receives the death penalty for his betrayal. [Credit: UPI/Bettmann Newsphotos]

Cuba got Shelepin into trouble for a second and final time. When the idea of putting nuclear missiles in Cuba was first proposed, Shelepin was wary of it, thinking it would enrage Kennedy. But the military assured Khrushchev that, after the Bay of Pigs debacle, Kennedy could be pushed around and wouldn't retaliate. Shelepin disagreed, but again was ignored. When the Red Army began to set up the Cuban missile bases, Shelepin protested strongly, and for his obstructionism, he was ousted as chief of the KGB in November 1961. In his place Khrushchev appointed Vladimir Yefimovich Semichastny.

Shelepin, of course, turned out to be right about the Cuban missiles; Kennedy couldn't be bullied and Khrushchev had to order the removal of the weapons. In a strange way, however, the crisis was good to both leaders. It gave Kennedy a chance to act tough, which made up in part for the Bay of Pigs. With the military proved wrong in its assessment, the crisis gave Khrushchev the chance to reduce the power of the Red Army. And, it opened up communications between the two world leaders. Both could boast of having a "special relationship" with the other leader and this gave each of them extra power and prestige within their own countries. Indeed, one can mark the beginning of the downfall of Khrushchev as November 22, 1963, the day President Kennedy was assassinated. From then on, Khrushchev no longer had his special prestige.

Khrushchev was ousted in 1964 by a coalition headed by Leonid Brezhnev and Alexei Kosygin, with the backing of the military. Semichastny, although an appointee of Khrushchev's, managed to survive the transition.

But, Semichastny made two mistakes that ended his career: he botched a reorganization of the air force; and he didn't foresee Stalin's daughter's defection to Britain. Semichastny had to pay. In April 1967 he was out, and in came the man who was to become the single most powerful chief of the organs since Beria. His name was Yuri Andropov.

We saw earlier how Andropov gained prominence with his handling of the Hungarian uprising in 1956. After that he continued to rise within KGB and party circles. His intelligence reports were widely respected in the Soviet hierarchy for their clarity and insight. In 1962 he received the distinction of being appointed secretary of the Central Committee. By the time he was appointed KGB chief in 1967 he had the experience, credentials, and connections to do the job.

Brezhnev had made a straightforward deal with the military—support him in his push to oust Khrushchev, and he and Kosygin would let the military expand and rearm to its heart's content. It was also part of the deal that the KGB had to remain apolitical and help the GRU in stealing military secrets. When Andropov became KGB chief he agreed to these conditions. In exchange he received Brezhnev's full support. As Brezhnev's star ascended in the 1970s—Kosygin becoming more and more peripheral—so did Andropov's.

From the Soviet point of view, Andropov was undoubtedly the most successful head of the organs since Dzerzhinsky. Andropov required and received total loyalty and respect. He rejected cronyism, only promoting the best, the brightest, and the toughest. He took thorough personal control of the KGB and revitalized it. Brezhnev's regime was shot through with corruption, but little of this reached Andropov's KGB. The organs had not been this strong or this powerful since the days of Beria, and nor had its chief. Andropov was the first head of the organs since Beria to be invited to join the Politburo.

In 1982, Leonid Brezhnev died. Andropov then succeeded where Beria had tried so hard and failed—he became the leader of the Soviet Union.

6.

THE KGB TODAY—THE ANDROPOV LEGACY

In the 1950s and 1960s, Soviet Premier Nikita Khrushchev tried to change the image of the KGB so that Soviet citizens wouldn't be so terrified that they stopped informing on their fellow citizens. As part of this clean-up campaign, the organs began to celebrate the great heroes of Soviet espionage—the likes of Richard Sorge and Colonel Rudolph Abel—and the spies who had betrayed the West—the likes of Donald Maclean and Kim Philby.

Twenty years later, this popularization continued. The year 1987 marked the 70th anniversary of the creation of the Cheka and in honor of that most auspicious occasion, the KGB commissioned plays, movies, books, and art that celebrated the history of the organs.

This is strange even to the most passive observer because the history of the Soviet organs is a history of blood and terror, leavened only slightly by the back-stabbing antics of its power-mad leaders. It is also strange because such open acknowledgment of espionage conflicts with the secrecy usually associated with spying. It is not something that would be considered in the West. In Britain, the secret services, MI6 (foreign intelligence gathering) and MI5 (counterintelligence), are not to be talked about officially. In the United States, 1987 marked the CIA's 40th anniversary but there were no art contests or public celebrations.

But for all the celebrations and awards given to its spies, still very little is known about the KGB. We've looked at its history, we've seen who did what when, but what is it really like inside the Commission for State Security?

It's not easy to find out such things. It's the KGB's job to protect the secrets of the Soviet Union, and the secrets it protects most jealously are those involving its own operations. Still, we do know some things about its structure and operation.

DZERZHINSKY SQUARE

KGB headquarters are located on Dzerzhinsky Square in the heart of Moscow. The square is named after Felix Dzerzhinsky, first head of the Cheka. The main building, at 2 Dzerzhinsky Square, was the headquarters of an insurance company before the revolution. Much of the additional building was constructed by political prisoners and German prisoners of war after World War II. There is an interior courtyard to the complex, one wall of which is formed by Lubyanka Prison, scene of countless executions during the numerous purges of the last 70 years. The KGB has other buildings—the First Directorate is just outside of Moscow and the GRU has its headquarters in the old Khodina airfield in the middle of Moscow—but Dzerzhinsky Square is the heart of the KGB and is known as "The Center."

The chairman of the KGB has his office on the third floor of the main building. Most other officers of the Collegium—the executive branch of the KGB—also have their offices on this floor. The chairman's office is nothing lavish, but it does demonstrate the perks of privilege—foreign consumer goods most especially—that go with the job. On the desk there is a row of phones. One is a direct link to the Kremlin, the seat of power in the Soviet Union.

According to the Soviet rules of government, the KGB is supposed to report to the Council of Ministers. This would be the rough equivalent of the cabinet in the United States. However, in practice, the KGB is first responsible to the communist party, for it is the party that rules the country (and, in any event, everyone elected to office in the govern-

KGB Organization

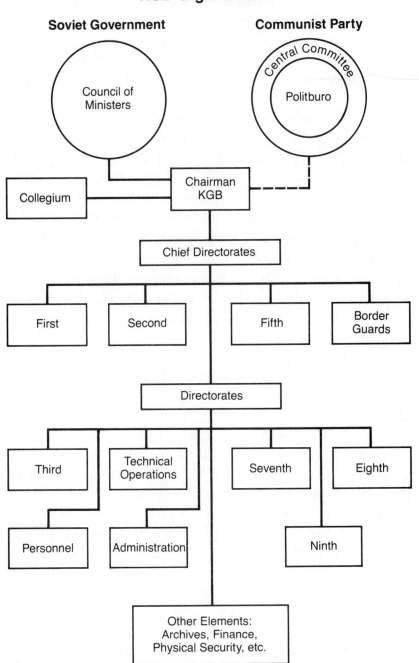

Note: Although according to Soviet Law the KGB is governed by the Council of Ministers, it is in fact controlled by the CPSU.

ment and all the ministers are all members of the party). For this reason, the chairman of the KGB also has on his desk a phone line connecting him directly to the line the Politburo members use. All KGB actions are monitored very closely by the party. In effect, the watchdog of the party is itself closely watched.

The organization of the KGB is always in flux. Directorates change names, numbers, and responsibilities fairly often (partly in a search for greater efficiency, partly to confuse Western observers, but most often because of political machinations). One of the better outlines of the KGB's organization came out in the early 1970s. Although undoubtably some of the specifics have changed since then, the basic outline still probably holds true. Although many of the directorates are numbered, not all the numbers are used— for example, while there is a First, Second, and Fifth Directorate, the Third is known by a different name and there is no Fourth.

Following the hierarchy from the top down, beneath the chairman and Collegium of the KGB are the four chief directorates—the First, Second, Fifth and Border Guards Directorates.

The First Chief Directorate. This is where KGB spies come from. Headquarters for the First Chief Directorate are located in a newer building (built in the 60s) just outside Moscow. Within the directorate there are three subdirectorates. Directorate S runs the "illegals"—the Soviet agents that are placed in a country illegally, undercover, as opposed to those who don't hide their Soviet citizenship and operate out of embassies, consulates, trade missions, etc. Directorate T, Science and Technology, is responsible for stealing high-technology secrets from the West, focusing primarily on computer, avionic, missile, and nuclear technology. Directorate I, Planning and Analysis, does little of importance and is basically a retirement home for aging KGB officers.

Organization of the First Chief Directorate

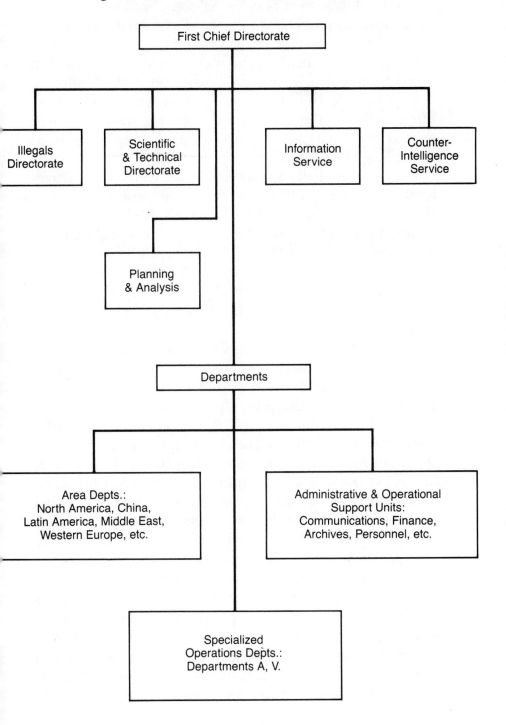

There are also two Special Services. Special Services I, Information, should be the source of intelligence estimates, but the KGB is so afraid of making a wrong estimate that it doesn't produce much in the way of refined analysis but instead sends nearly raw intelligence on to the Politburo. Special Service II, Counterintelligence, has the job of infiltrating the intelligence services of other countries, not only to find out what they are up to but to keep them from disrupting KGB operations.

The two special departments within the First Chief Directorate are perhaps the most infamous within the KGB. Department A, Disinformation, is responsible for disseminating misleading information around the world that will either cast the Soviet Union in a favorable light or throw mud on its opponents. Department V, Executive Action, is where those spy-film villains would really come from. Department V agents handle the really dirty work, the *mokrie dela*, or "wet affairs."

The remainder of the First Chief Directorate is divided into departments that divvy up the world for operations. The first 10 departments are oriented geographically—the First Department handles the United States and Canada; the Second Department handles the United Kingdom, Australia, New Zealand, and Scandinavia; and so on. The last six departments cover special operational areas such as finding cover jobs or managing relations with the intelligence services of Cuba and the Eastern bloc, or creating forged passports and other documents needed by the spies.

The Second Chief Directorate. The Second Chief Directorate runs all operations against foreigners in the Soviet Union, whether to recruit them as spies or compromise them in some way. If you're a journalist with your newspaper's Moscow bureau, you'll be targeted by the agents of this chief directorate. These agents are also responsible for monitoring and preventing any contact between Soviet citizens and foreigners. There is a Technical Support Group within the Second Chief Directorate that specializes in burglary—

breaking into embassies to plant bugs, steal code books, and the like.

The Border Guards are crack troops, an elite crop created in Lenin's day. Their job is not so much to keep people from getting into the Soviet Union—although they had to do that during the Soviet-Chinese border skirmishes of the late 60s and early 70s—but to prevent people from escaping. There are 300,000 troops in the Border Guards directorate.

The Fifth Directorate is where the "men-in-black" come from. It is the job of these agents to suppress all opposition and dissent within the Soviet Union. This directorate focuses primarily on dissidents, Jewish "refuseniks" (so-called because their requests to emigrate to Israel have been refused by the state) and nationalists. Let us not forget that less than half of the Soviet Union is populated by Russians. The remainder are people of other nations, roped into the Soviet Union, most against their will. It is the job of the agents of the Fifth Directorate to crush nationalist sentiment in such places as Armenia, Lithuania, the Ukraine, and the republics of Central Asia.

Beneath these chief directorates are the remaining seven directorates. The *Armed Forces Directorate* (also known as the Third Directorate) is required to spy on the members of the military, to make sure that no one strays from the fold. This is the descendant of the infamous Osobyi Otdel, the OO that followed behind the Red Army during the civil war and shot stragglers. The *Technical Operations Directorate* makes all the spy gadgets and dirty-tricks paraphernalia, from bugs to poison pens. The *Administration Directorate* handles the day-to-day business of running the KGB. As in any bureaucracy, the department that handles hiring, firing, training, and promotion carries a great deal of weight, and so it is for the KGB's *Personnel Directorate*.

The *Seventh Directorate*, the Surveillance Directorate, employs several thousand agents who have one job— following people around throughout the Soviet Union. The

Eighth Directorate handles the enormous task of communications intelligence—making codes and ciphers to protect Soviet communications and breaking the codes and ciphers of other nations. The *Ninth Directorate* is the equivalent of the US Secret Service. These are the guards that protect the members of the ruling elite. The agents of the Ninth Directorate are the most closely scrutinized of all KGB agents, and the most highly trained. They are the only people in the Soviet Union allowed to carry weapons near members of the Politburo.

There are also numerous other departments in the KGB, handling everything from finance to registry and archives.

There are roughly 90,000 officers working for the KGB worldwide, with another 400,000 support personnel (this includes the Border Guards). Including recruited spies and informers, the KGB probably employs up to 2 million people around the globe.

Who are these people?

A LIFE IN THE KGB

In the United States you'll see a CIA employment opportunities ad in the major city newspapers from time to time. You won't see such an ad in *Pravda,* the Soviet Communist Party newspaper. Joining the KGB is like joining a secret society at an Ivy League college—you don't ask to join, they ask you. If you're asked to join the KGB, it is wise to accept.

It's smart for a Soviet citizen to accept the KGB's tap on the shoulder, not only because refusing doesn't look good but because working for the KGB provides one with much prestige and many privileges.

Prestige! It may be hard for those of us in the West to imagine anything prestigious about working for the KGB, but it's a different matter in Russia. In the Soviet Union spies are true heroes. Men who recruit traitors in the United States get their pictures in the paper, perhaps even a medal (*after* a successful operation, of course).

Certainly Soviet citizens are not keen on having secret policemen watching their every move, and yet they have been so indoctrinated in the need for vigilance against the internal threat of counterrevolutionaries that working for the KGB, even for the internal security wings, does not carry a stigma. And, if one gets a job with the First Chief Directorate—as a real spy—there is actual, palpable prestige.

But what can be even more attractive are the privileges. KGB officers don't have to wait in line at the GUM stores (state-run supermarkets and department stores) for a few eggs; they get their choice of fresh fruit, vegetables, and meat. They also get a crack at owning foreign consumer goods that other citizens never see. Best of all, they get the chance to travel outside the Soviet Union.

It's this last privilege, the occasional opportunity to see the world, that also causes the KGB so much trouble, for the agents who leave the country as spies are the most vulnerable to being "turned" (recruited as double agents) by foreign intelligence services. For this reason, the KGB recruits as much as it can from the families of agents; it makes checking the person's past and loyalty that much easier. Also, when they do send an agent abroad, the KGB tries to send agents with wives and families who remain in the Soviet Union, as they can be used as insurance that the agent will return.

The highest status jobs in the KGB are those that involve being posted to an embassy, consulate, or trade organization under "legal" cover. The Soviets employ these legal agents as much as they are allowed to get away with by the host countries. In 1971 there were 809 people from various countries with diplomatic accreditation in Moscow, while the Soviets had 1,769 such diplomats placed in those various countries. There are also thousands upon thousands of KGB agents who work abroad under cover of Aeroflot, the Soviet airline, and for trade organizations.

Getting a foreign posting isn't enough, however. There are good countries and there are bad countries. To a KGB officer, being sent to Beijing is good but being sent to Tokyo is bad. Sound strange? Well, it's almost impossible to set up spy networks in China, so very little is expected of an officer there, whereas it's relatively easy to work in Japan so much more is expected. KGB officers don't want hard work because they don't want to fail. Failing means being sent home to an uncertain future.

One of the main jobs of a legal KGB agent—as it is for a similar agent in the CIA or any intelligence service—is to recruit foreigners to work for them.

Recruiting spies is of paramount importance to the Soviets. The KGB enjoys the fruits of spy satellites and other technical methods of intelligence gathering as much as the US does, but they thrive on HUMINT—HUMan-gathered INTelligence. They don't care much for research intelligence, such as piecing together an idea of what Lockheed is up to through trade publications and other available material. They want to have someone inside Lockheed giving them hard information about the new stealth spy plane Kelly Johnson is building.

In the 1960s, a Western intelligence agency managed to procure a Soviet training manual on how to recruit agents. Produced by the Higher Intelligence School 101, it is called "The Practice of Recruiting Americans in the USA and Third Countries." It details the very straightforward but effective approach the KGB and GRU officers (for the GRU does the lion's share of recruiting in the military intelligence field) use to hook people into spying for Russia.

The KGB manual outlines the basic steps legals and illegals take to recruit spies. The potential spy is first spotted and identified. The KGB is looking for people who have a personal grudge—perhaps they have been passed over for a promotion or they don't like their boss. They are wary of using people who are ideologically motivated; they might change their minds. They want people who are in for the money, or to get even, or both. After a potential spy has been spotted, casual contact is made—the officer hangs out at the person's favorite bookstore or coffee shop and strikes up a conversation. The officer's goal is to establish rapport, the beginnings of a friendship.

When the officer and the potential spy are buddies, the officer will ask the fellow for some material that is legally available and will insist on paying for it. The KGB wants to establish as early as possible the pattern of materials for money. Then, if all that goes well, the officer will ask for some classified material. If the recruit goes along with this and takes money for it, he's hooked. He can't back out easily now—the KGB has a record of him taking money that they could use to expose him.

In the final step, the officer sees how the recruit reacts to the idea of working for the Soviets. If he agrees, the Soviets have a new spy. If he balks, the Soviets will threaten to expose the recruit, but will probably just cut their losses and run.

Recruitment is not easy. Two things make it especially hard. For one, few people want to work for the Soviets. So, as mentioned in the previous chapter, the KGB will use its "brothers"—agents of other Soviet bloc security agencies—to make the pitch. The other problem is recruiting within the United States; the FBI does its job very well. That's why recruitment is often attempted outside of the United States, when people are stationed in other countries or when they are visiting the Soviet Union. Most Intourist—the Soviet state tour agency that guides visitors through the USSR—representatives work for the KGB, spotting potential spies.

It should also be remembered that not all recruits are voluntary. The KGB will gladly blackmail or extort someone into spying for them.

The most prestigious KGB assignment in terms of danger and excitement is undoubtably that of the "illegal." These are agents who live in deep cover around the world. Their training is the most elaborate and extensive of all KGB foreign service agents. It can take years to prepare an illegal to take his or her position abroad. They are often sent to their host country in steps, moving from one country to another, establishing a "legend," a story that they can use. Then, once their identity is established, they may surreptitiously return to the Soviet Union for another year or two of training.

When they are finally put in place they do not do any spying themselves; they recruit others. They will often take a job that allows them mobility and freedom and a variety of contacts. Gordon Lonsdale rented jukeboxes; Rudolph Abel was a painter—both perfect occupations for someone who may need to move around a lot and who won't keep regular hours.

They all have to prepare for the possibility of being betrayed or otherwise uncovered. Illegals usually have some sort of fall-back story. A popular one has the spy admit that he is not who his passport says he is. He will break down, saying he is a criminal who escaped from Romania. Romania will concur that he is a bad, bad man and whisk him off. Of course the spy is not Romanian, but he will be back, safe behind the Iron Curtain.

Illegals may go for years and decades without being detected. Indeed, it must be assumed that most do escape detection. There are likely thousands of Soviet illegals operating in the United States at this point in time.

There is one other employment opportunity that bears examination—that of a practitioner of *mokrie dela*, wet work. This has always been a disturbing question—who does the wet work?

A one-time head of the organs' wet affairs reportedly described who they should look for to do the *mokrie dela*: "Go search for people who are hurt by fate or nature—the ugly, those suffering from an inferiority complex, craving power and influence but defeated by unfavorable circumstances . . . The sense of belonging to an influential, powerful organization will give them a feeling of superiority . . . For the first time in their lives they will experience a sense of importance . . . It is sad indeed, and humanly shallow, but we are obliged to profit from it."

The amount of wet work conducted by the Soviets has changed over the years. It reached a kind of insane zenith in the years following World War II. At that time, the part of the organs responsible for wet work was the Special Bureau. The Special Bureau carried out an aggressive campaign of murder against any and all opponents. Large numbers of disgruntled émigrés were poisoned or gunned down in the streets of foreign cities.

Many bizarre methods of murder came out of the Camera (Kamera), a special laboratory that developed methods of killing people that would seem natural and poisons so dangerous that even the scientists that worked in the Camera were afraid to go inside the lab or touch anything.

One of the first things Khrushchev did after Beria was gone in 1953 was abolish the Special Bureau and the Camera. Of course the abolition was only temporary. Wet affairs reappeared in 1954 as part of Department 13 of the First Chief Directorate of the KGB. Western intelligence first became fully aware of the wet affairs department in 1954 when a Department 13 officer, Captain Nikolai Khoklov, defected. The KGB as a whole and Department 13 in particular does not take kindly to defections. In 1957, KGB agents tracked Khoklov down and poisoned him with thallium, a rare, highly toxic metal. Doctors tried every known antidote to thallium but none worked. Khoklov barely survived. It was later discovered that his old friends in the Camera had saturated the thallium with high-level radiation, a process which made it work faster and almost invulnerable to treatment.

The assassinations of Ukrainian émigrés carried out by Stashinsky for the most part marked the end of KGB agents killing people. From the early 1960s on, liquidations by KGB operatives were sharply curtailed—at least by their own officers. Now they do other things, like plan for sabotage.

In 1971, Oleg Lyalin, a Department V operative, defected to the British. His defection led to the expulsion of 105 KGB agents in England. It also led to widespread panic among

Department V operatives around the world, dozens of whom were recalled to Moscow for fear that Lyalin had betrayed them. Most of these agents were involved in stockpiling weaponry and explosives and planning acts of sabotage in case war came. There are probably dozens of such agents in the United States today.

For assassinations, the KGB has in recent years turned to its brothers in the Bulgarian secret police. On September 7, 1978, Georgi Markov, a Bulgarian defector, was walking over the Waterloo Bridge in London when he felt a sharp stabbing pain in his thigh. He looked to see a man with an umbrella apologizing profusely for having accidentally poked him. Markov thought nothing of it at the time, but later that night he became gravely ill, and four days later he died.

The man on the bridge had been an agent of the Bulgarian secret police, and the umbrella tip contained a miniature air gun that fired a pellet containing an exotic poison deep into Markov's thigh. The pellet was so small it was almost missed in the autopsy.

The Bulgarians could have killed Markov in any number of ways, several of which could have appeared to have been accidental. But they didn't want it to look like an accident. They wanted the message to get out to all defectors that they might be killed at any time.

The question of defectors is a difficult one for the KGB. KGB agents are more likely to defect than other citizens because they get the chance to live outside the USSR. When a KGB legal defects, a whole procedure comes into play.

When a KGB officer in a foreign country is missing, the first thing that the local Soviet ambassador and KGB resident hope for is that the man is dead, and so, the morgues and hospitals are checked. Then they use informants to see if the man is being held on some criminal charge, whether it's car theft or espionage. At this stage of the game they tell the host country of the man's disappearance and say they suspect foul play. After 24 hours they start attacking the host country's inability to restrain anti-Soviet activity.

When they find out that the man has defected, they shift gears. They call him a criminal, a pervert, a molester, a rapist—anything to cast doubt on the deserter. They might even turn up some heat on the host country's embassy in Moscow—there might suddenly be an unruly demonstration outside the embassy.

The Soviets then demand to see the man. The host country will give in, but will set élaborate security precautions so that the man is not abducted. The Soviets agree. When they go see the defector they will be excessively friendly, as if seeing a long lost chum. Then, in quiet voices, they will tell the man of his relatives' concerns back in Russia. If that doesn't move him they will be more blunt—the deserter should expect to be looking over his shoulder for the rest of his life. And, finally, if that fails to move the deserter, the Soviets will carefully, over the next little while, plant seeds of doubt in the minds of Western intelligence that the deserter may be a double agent.

Often, the KGB can't get a deserter to come home. Occasionally they can. In the summer of 1985, Vitaly Yurchenko, a 25-year KGB veteran, defected to the United States. Later that year, he changed his mind—probably after receiving some communication from the KGB—and bolted from the men assigned to take care of him while they were having dinner at a restaurant in Georgetown.

There are, of course, countless other job opportunities within the KGB. All in all, in terms of the lot of the average Soviet citizen, a life in the KGB is not at all a bad one. Sure, some assignments may not be entirely pleasant (spying on your fellow citizens) but you do get fresh fruit and the possibility of owning a VCR.

THE ANDROPOV LEGACY

We discussed in the introduction how the organs are a part of the entirety of Russian history and that they were not an invention of the Bolsheviks. True enough. Yet, as much as the KGB is just the most recent incarnation of the organs, it is also in some ways unique to the Soviet regime, for no version of the organs has ever been as powerful as the KGB. It is so large, so inextricably entwined throughout Soviet society and politics, that in some ways it is easier to imagine the KGB existing on its own without the rest of the Soviet state than it is to imagine the present Soviet state existing without the KGB.

Some believe Lenin never saw the Cheka as only a temporary necessity, but that he planned all along to keep it in some form or another long after the Bolsheviks had secured their rule. Even if he truly did first conceive of it as temporary, he and his followers quickly became aware that in order to maintain a totalitarian state—or "dictatorship of the proletariat"—they needed an organ to effect that total control. The fear was that without that control, the Soviet state would fall apart.

Maintaining such control in any country is a daunting task; in a country the size of the Soviet Union, it's an awesome job, carrying with it, for the survival of the state, a tremendous responsibility. With such responsibility, however, comes power, and the KGB's power makes it one of the three ruling forces in Russia.

The triad of the Soviet state consists of the communist party, the Red Army, and the KGB. The party is supposed to be the first among equals, and the Red Army is supposed to have greater power than the KGB. But that hierarchy—party, army, KGB—has not always been in place, nor is it today. Under Josef Stalin, while the party retained its supremacy, the Red Army's status dropped, and the organs grew in stature.

In Stalin's day, the second most powerful man in the Soviet Union was the head of the organs, Lavrenti Beria, who became known as the most feared man in the country. Once Stalin and Beria were gone, one of Khrushchev's first items of business was to attempt to restructure the government so that never again could one man at the head of the organs achieve such power. He was successful—for a time.

In 1982 Yuri Andropov became the first head of the organs to rise to the position of leader of the Soviet Union. Brezhnev's regime was noted for its widespread corruption and the amount of power it gave to the Red Army. (Those were the years of the Soviets' massive arms buildups.) Andropov aimed to reverse all of that, ridding the Party and government of corruption and reducing the power of the military while at the same time reinforcing and strengthening the KGB's position.

Upon his death in 1984, Andropov was succeeded by Constantin Chernenko. But Chernenko was an aging, ailing, old-time party hack and his appointment as general secretary was just a temporary fix until one of Andropov's younger colleagues could be maneuvered into position to take over the party leadership. Indeed, when Chernenko died, the man who succeeded him had been closely allied with Andropov. His name, of course, is Mikhail Gorbachev.

Gorbachev's rather radical policies of *glasnóst* (the new openness) and *perestroika* (economic restructuring, allowing small measures of free enterprise) are, in some ways, a continuation of Andropov's agenda. They should then be seen in light of the ongoing, seemingly never-ending power struggle in the Soviet Union. Gorbachev's agenda goes further than Andropov's anti-corruption campaign, however, and his actions have pitted him against the status quo of the party elite. He can do this because he has the backing of the younger members of the party and the military. More importantly—and hardly ever mentioned—like Andropov, he has the backing of the KGB.

The Andropov legacy continues. When Gorbachev took over the leadership of the country, the head of the KGB was Victor Chebrikov. Chebrikov was a friend of Andropov who rose with him, from the days of Andropov's suppressing the 1956 Hungarian uprising on. By all indications, Chebrikov shared Andropov's goals and was following in the path that his mentor charted. Nevertheless, on October 1, 1988, as part of a huge shake up, Gorbachev named Chebrikov to head a new Central Committee commission on legal policy. In his place as KGB chief, Gorbachev appointed Vladimir Kryuchkov.

Kryuchkov is not an outsider. Although he was promoted over two more senior deputies, he is still a veteran. He joined the KGB in 1967, the year Andropov became chief, and his career was aided through the years by Andropov. By all indications, therefore, Kryuchkov, like Chebrikov—and Gorbachev for that matter—came from the Andropov camp. It doesn't seem that Kryuchkov's appointment signals a change in direction for the KGB. It seems more likely that Gorbachev simply wanted his own man, someone he could count on, at the head of the secret police.

What will happen in the Soviet Union remains to be seen. Gorbachev's attempts at reform may not succeed and he may be ousted by conservatives. If he does succeed, however, it will be because he can count the KGB on his side. As it stands now, the KGB is in a very favorable position. That could change, and, knowing Soviet history, it most probably will, as the never-ending struggle between the party, the Red Army, and the organs continues. For now, however, the sword and shield of the party has more power than the party itself. Today, the red star of the Soviet empire shines very brightly on Dzerzhinsky Square.

SUGGESTED READING

Barron, John. *KGB: The Secret Work of Soviet Secret Agents.* New York: Bantam Books, 1974.

————*KGB Today: The Hidden Hand.* New York: Reader's Digest Press, 1983.

Bledowskia, Celina and Bloch, Jonathan. *KGB/CIA* New York: Exeter Books, 1987.

Deacon, Richard. *A History of the Russian Secret Service.* London: Grafton Books, 1987.

Deriabin, Peter. *Watchdogs of Terror.* New York: Arlington House, 1972.

Dziak, John J. *Chekisty: A History of the KGB.* Lexington, Mass.: Lexington Books, 1987.

Corson, William R. and Crowley, Robert T. *The New KGB.* New York: William Morrow and Company, 1985.

Freemantle, Brian. *KGB.* New York: Holt, Rinehart and Winston, 1982.

Lindsey, Robert. *The Falcon and the Snowman.* New York: Pocket Books, 1980.

Suvorov, Viktor. *Inside Soviet Military Intelligence.* New York: Macmillan Publishing Company, 1984.

Wise, David and Ross, Thomas B., *The Espionage Establishment.* New York: Random House, 1967.

Yost, Graham. *Spy-Tech.* New York: Facts On File, 1985.

INDEX